Killing Black Innocents

The Program to Control "African American" Reproduction (from Slavery's End to the Present-Day *Self-Inflicted* Genocide)

ELISHA J. ISRAEL

Copyright © 2012 Elisha J. Israel

All rights reserved.

DEDICATION

God is the source of my strength, and my protection. I thank the Lord for all that I am, all that I am able to do, and any good that is within me. To my mother who almost died giving birth to me and sacrificed her life for me, to my best friend, confidant, and wife Naomi who has given me beautiful children, To my grandmother who has been a pillar of strength and shown me nothing but love, to my Aunts Gloria, Sonja, and Hilda who have nurtured me like second mothers, and to Sister Anna who has treated me like a son.

CONTENTS

1	Control of Black Reproduction During Slavery	1
2	The Negro Problem and the Emergence of Eugenics	10
3	Margaret Sanger and the Negro Project	22
4	The "Rhineland Bastardes" of Germany	38
5	The Mississippi Appendectomy	43
6	"Welfare Queens", Teens and "Crack Mommas" Need Birth Control!	51
7	Birth Control and Black Leadership (From Garvey to Obama)	58
8	Why Roe v. Wade is Unconstitutional	70
9	Biblical Argument Against Abortion	84
10	Appeal to Conscience: Abortion A Part of a Larger Problem	91
	Bibliography	115

INTO EGYPT AGAIN WITH SHPS: A MESSAGE TO THE FORGOTTEN ISRAELITES (AFRICAN AMERICANS)

by Elisha J. Israel©
NOW AVAILABLE ON-LINE @ **ISRAELTEACH.COM, AMAZON.COM BARNES & NOBLE.COM**

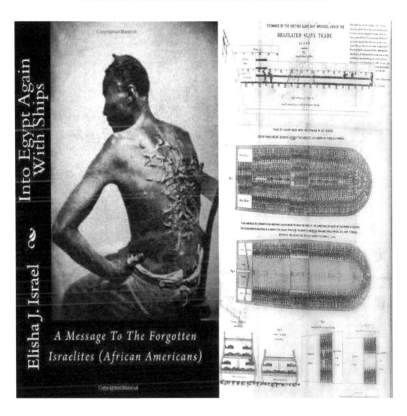

INTO EGYPT AGAIN WITH SHIPS explains the spiritual implications regarding more that 250 years of chattel slavery, 100 years of Jim Crow, semi-permanent underclass status, and loss of true identity that "African Americans" have suffered in the United States. This book also reveals the biblical solution that will lead to the complete liberation of a people. All those who have descended from slaves, and consider themselves to be "Negro", "Black", or "African American" should have the audacity to read this book.

1
CONTROL OF REPRODUCTION DURING SLAVERY

Prior to entering into the Promised Land, Moses foretold of Israel's captivity as a consequence of disobedience. The prophet writes:

> And the Lord shall bring thee into Egypt again with ships, by the way whereof I spake unto thee, Thou shalt see it no more again: and there ye shall be sold unto your enemies for bondmen and bondwomen, and no man shall buy you.[1]

Moses prophesied that the children of Israel would be taken into slavery by way of cargo slave ships and then sold as bondmen and bondwomen.[2] This prophecy was fulfilled with the emergence of the Transatlantic Slave Trade. It is estimated that between the 16th and 19th centuries approximately 645,000 black slaves were transported by way of slave ships to what became the United States of America. In 1790, the slave population was under 800,000. The year 1808 marked the end of this legal importation of slaves from Africa through the Atlantic Slave Trade. However, after this point there was a tremendous increase in the number of bondmen and bondwomen in the U.S. The slave population increased from 1,191,362[3] in 1810 to 3,953,760 in 1860.[4] Some historians argue that this increase was merely a natural increase in the birth rate. However, it is likely that this swelling was, at least in part, a consequence of slave breeding. The extent to which breeding was utilized among slave owners has been a point of contestation among historians. But it is certain that after 1808, the year in which slave importation became illegal in the U.S., the system of slavery was sustained through childbearing. Furthermore, it is a fact that the slave's offspring was the property of the owner. Consequently it was undoubtedly beneficial for a master to encourage intercourse between male and female slaves.

Planters realized very early during the era of slavery that although women were valuable laborers alongside men their principal asset rested in their ability to reproduce. Thomas Jefferson, who as president signed the bill prohibiting slave importation, considered a female slave who birthed a child every two years to be more valuable than the best male field hand.[5] Advertisements and articles during the slave era often emphasized the fertility of female slaves as a selling point. For instance, an advertisement in the Charleston Mercury of May 16, 1838, read: "A GIRL about 20 years of age… She is remarkably strong and healthy… She is a prolific in her generating qualities, and affords a rare opportunity for any person who wishes to raise a family of strong and healthy servants…"[6] Frederick Douglass, the abolitionist and former slave, stated that his master Mr. Covey bought a woman named Caroline for the purpose of breeding.[7]

Upper Slave States

What occurred after in the Upper South 1808 should also be considered as indication of slave breeding. Much of the wealth in the Upper Southern states derived from the sale of human capital. The ban on slave importation caused the price of slaves to increase tremendously in these states. Those in the Upper South soon understood that the value of their slaves was in what their counterparts in the Lower South were willing to pay. Slave labor was in great demand and the greatest potential to gain wealth through labor was in the cotton growing states. As a result, slave owners of the Upper South were encouraged to breed their slaves rather than allow them to rear families through marriage naturally. In an 1829 speech before the Kentucky Colonization Society, Henry Clay stated that "the Upper South would not employ slave labor if it were not for the temptation to raise slaves by the high price of the Southern markets... which keeps it up in their own." Olmstead concluded the following after his travels through the South:

> In the states of Maryland, Virginia, North Carolina, Kentucky, Tennessee, as much attention is paid to the breeding and growth of negroes as to that of horses and mules. Further south, we raise them both for use and for market. Planters command their girls and women (married or unmarried) to have children; and I have known a great many girls to be sold off because they did not have children. A breeding woman is worth from one-sixth to one-forth more than one that does not breed.[8]

Virginia, a state in the soil had been exhausted by tobacco, became known not only for breeding horses, but Negroes as well. Thomas Dew of William and Mary College maintained that Viriginia was "in fact a negro raising state for other states, it is one of their greatest sources of profit."[9] To prove the occurrence of slave breeding, John Elliot Cairnes, a protégé of John Stuart Mill, pointed to the inconsistency in the number of young adult slaves. He argued:

> Now these are facts which no mere migration of population will account for. If a planter with his family and its following of slaves, removed from Virginia to Arkansas, the young and the old of both races would go together... But where slave dealing prevails in connexion with slave-breeding, this cannot happen... It is plain that nothing less than a regular systematic traffic in human beings could produce such results as these in the vital statistics of a nation.[10]

Some scholars even maintain that stud farms existed in the Upper South during slavery.[11] A.H. Conrad and J.R. Meyer argued that stud farms may have existed primarily for two reasons. The Upper South had remarkably higher ratios of fertility, which suggests successful breeding. In addition, the price of female slaves in these states was especially high, which may indicate that females were coveted for their potential to breed. Sutch observed that among slaves exported from the Upper South, males were approximately 7 percent more numerous than female slaves, which may indicate that females were maintained as breeding slaves. Sutch also utilized census evidence to pinpoint a number of possible stud farms.

Stockmen & Breeding Women

Although it is quite difficult to substantiate beyond a shadow of doubt the existence of stud farms, there were men of exceptional build and physical prowess who were used specifically for the purpose of breeding. These "breedin' niggers", "travelin' niggers", or "stockmen" as they were called, were, according to one slave, "weighed, rented, and then put in a room with some young woman a slave owner wanted to raise children from."[12] Jeptha Choice described his role as a stockman as follows: "When I was young they took care not to strain me and I was as handsome as a speckled pup and was in demand for breedin."[13] Elgie Davison, who also fulfilled the role of stud, stated that his master required him to take fifteen wives and father children. Davison was unsure of the exact number of children that he fathered, but he was certain that the number exceeded one hundred.[14] According to some accounts hese men were often prevented from an abundance of strenuous labor. Willie Williams, a former Louisiana slave, stated the following concerning a "stockman" owned by his master: "Dat nigger do no work but watch dem womens and he am de husband for dem all. De master sho' was a-raisin' some fine niggers dat way.[15] Because of the economic risk, some owners went as far as to castrate male slaves that they considered unfit to breed. Cornelia Andres, a slave of North Carolina, witnessed this barbarity. She said, "Yo' knows dey ain't lat no little runty nigger have no chilluns. Naw sir, dey ain't, dey operate on dem lak dey does male hogs so's dat dey can't have no little runty chilluns;"[16]

Slave owners often matched males and females for the sole purpose of producing the "best stock". Jacob Branch, a former slave of Texas, tells of how enslaved men and women were paired together to breed:

> Massa go buy a cullud man name Uncle Charley Fenner. Hea good old cullud man. Massa brung him to de quarters and say, "Renee, here you husband," and den he turn to Uncle and say, "Charley, dis you woman." Den dey consider dem married. Dat de way de marry den, by de massa's word.[17]

Women were expected to bear children from these relationships or suffer the severe consequences. Louisa "Nor" Everett recalls the gross way in which a husband was chosen for her:

> Marse Jim called me and Sam ter him and ordered Sam to pull off his shirt- that was all the McClain niggers wore-and he said to me: "Nor, do you think you can stand this big nigger?" He had that old bullwhip flung acrost his shoulder, and Lawd, that man could hit so hard! So I jes' said "yassur, I guess so," and tried to hide my face so I couldn't see Sam's nakedness, but he made me look at him anyhow. Well, he told us what we must git busy and do in his presence, and we had to do it. After that we was considered man and wife. Me and Same was a healthy pair and had fine big babies, so I never had another man forced on me, thank God. Sam was kind to me and I learned to love him.[18]

Female slaves who were able to bear children had high value in the market and were less likely to be sold. In many instances bearing children ensured that a young woman would not be sold and separated from her family. Some bondswomen offered certain "rewards" for women such as better clothing, hair ribbons, extra rations, relief from work, small amounts of money, and even promises of freedom.[19] It is not hard to fathom, when one considers the abuses invoked upon slaves for minor infractions, that male and female slaves would be forced to breed by threat of physical force. Nehemiah Caulkins tells the following account concerning an owner's fury over his female slave's failure to multiply:

> One day the owner ordered the women into the barn, he then went in among them, whip in hand, and told them he meant to flog them all to death; they began immediately to cry out "What have I done Massa?" He replied; "Damn you, I will let you know what you have done, you don't breed, I haven't had a young one from you for several months.[20]

In this particular instance the bondwomen informed their slave master that due to the nature of work in the rice ditches they were unable to breed. The work required them to toil in mud and water between one to two feet in depth. After more threats this owner allowed for the women to be given work on land when they were pregnant. Masters, who realized the economic benefits of ability to breed, often reduced the workloads and physical punishments of pregnant and post partum females. *The American Cotton Planter* suggested that women with children be "well treated and cared for, and moderately worked... their natural increase becomes a source of great profit to their owner. Whatever therefore tends to promote their health and render them prolific is worthy of his (the slave owner's) attention."[21] John Calhoun stated that "Over-work produces premature old age, bodily deformity and debility of constitution, and checks the increase of females."[22]

However, there were many masters who considered not the potential for or expectation of children. One slave told of a master who scourged his pregnant slaves "with raw hide so that the blood and milk flew mingled from their breasts."[23] On many plantations women were required to resume manual labor soon after delivery. Often after delivery, slave women were unable to properly care for their children. Motherhood did not relieve her of the strenuous physical toils on the plantation. Many women were not only denied time to recuperate from childbirth but were forced to take their children to the fields with them. Infants were strapped to bodies and breast fed while mothers labored in the field. Others left their children with caregivers who were usually older slaves. Some female slaves made crude cradles in the ground nearby where they worked. Ida Hutchinson gives the following sorrowful account:

> Blacksheer had them take their babies with them to the field and it was two or three miles from the house to the field. He didn't want them to lose time walking backward and forward nursing. They built a long trough like a great long cradle and put all these babies in it every morning when the mother come out of the field. It was set at the end of the row, all at once a cloud no bigger than a small spot came up and it grew fast, and it thundered and lightened as if the world were coming to an end, and the rain just came down in great sheets. And when it got so they could go to the other end of the field, the trough was filled with water and every baby in it was floating round in the water, drowned. They never got narry a lick of labor and nary red penny for any of them babies.[24]

The death of infants born in slavery was quite common. In 1850 the infant mortality rate among slaves was twice that of white infants.[25] High morality rates were largely due to disease and malnutrition. To increase the chances of survival, it was not uncommon for bondwomen to plan pregnancies around labor cycles. Female slaves were more likely to get pregnant during times of decreased labor obligations. After the fall harvest, female slaves were able to consume healthier diets and in some cases carry their children during time of less disease. However, this was not always true. Many women endured the late stages of pregnancy during the most strenuous work cycles.

Resistance

As an act of resistance, some female slaves simply refused to bear children. Some planters complained to physicians of the "unnatural tendency in the African female to destroy her offspring and that whole families of women fail to have children." Reports reveal that slave owners complained to physicians convinced that female slaves knew of a "secret" method to destroy the fetus in the womb. The physician John T. Morgan reported to the Rutherford County Medical Society in 1860 that slave women implemented several techniques to avoid conception which included violent exercise and external and internal manipulation. Morgan also stated that herbs such as tansy, rue, roots and seed, cotton plant, pennyroyal, cedar gum, and camphor were used to induce abortion.[26]

Rape

Black female slaves were considered to be mere property and had little power to prevent the sexual advances of white male slave owners. The legal system did not protect the bondwoman from sexual assault, thus masters were able to commit heinous sexual acts with impunity. Slave-children were also susceptible to rape by slave masters.[27] Linda Brent described the experience of slave girls as follows: "When she is fourteen or fifteen her owner or his sons or the overseer or perhaps all of them begin to bribe her with presents. If these fail to accomplish their purpose, she is whipped or starved into submission to their will."[28] Although rape certainly fulfilled the master's licentious desire, lust was not the sole purpose. Rape is an act of *power*. Rape reinforced the subjugation of the female slave. It also served to emasculate the male slave who was unable to protect his mother, wife, sister, or daughter. Louisa "Nor" Everett stated that not only did her master have sex with the slaves, but so did his guests. According to Sam and Louisa Everett, husbands were required to watch as their wives were raped.[29] The prophet Moses predicted that during Israel's captivity this would occur when he wrote, "Thou shalt betroth a wife, and another man shall lie with her..."[30] Rape often led to pregnancy and consequentially increased the number of slaves owned by a master. And, although there were substantially higher numbers of mulattos in the free black population, having "mixed blood" did not ensure freedom. In many slave states slave status was based on the status of the mother, not the father. Often mulatto slaves served as house servants while others toiled just like any other field hand. Simon Ansley Ferrall, in his travels through the South between 1829 and 1830, stated that it was "an occurrence of no uncommon nature to see the Christian father sell his own daughter".[31] Amy Elizabeth Patterson, a mulatto slave who was sold by her father, described this misdeed in the following words:

> That was the greatest crime ever visited on the United States. It was worse than the cruelty of oversees, worse than hunger... but when a father can sell his own child- humiliate his own daughter by auctioning her on the slave block- what good could be expected where such practices were allowed?... Yes, slavery is a curse to this nation, a curse which still shows itself in hundreds of homes where mulatto faces are evidence of a heinous sin, and proof that there has been a time when American fathers sold their children at the slave marts of America.[32]

Slaves born of white masters were coveted and commanded high prices in the market. Bondwomen of 'mixed' heritage were sold at the highest prices. It was also not uncommon for slaves owners to "improve stock" through rape. In *A Social History of the American Family*, Arthur Calhoun writes that college students from the North were paid by Southern slave owners to impregnate their female slaves.[33]

Jezebel-like Temptress

The Black female slave was depicted in total contrast to the Southern white "lady". The white woman represented purity and virtue, her womb was cherished. The bondwoman was stereotyped as a "Jezebel" who craved sexual pleasure indiscriminately. It was her spell, not the master's sinful lusts, which caused the slave master to yield. From this false perception of the female slave's willingness and desire to have the slave master meant two things. Not only did being a female slave mean suffering the most oppression (forced labor, sexual victimization, & forced breeding), it also meant that the female would be blamed for her own sexual abuse at the hands of the slave master. Bondwomen who bore the children of their masters often suffered the rage of their mistress. Embarrassed mistresses would often insist that slave children of the master be sold at the earliest prospect.

Prior to the end of slavery the manipulation of slave reproduction (through the forced pairing of male and female slaves as well as rape) was more than likely instrumental in swelling the Negro population to over 4 million. But once the Negro could no longer be lawfully enslaved, their presence became viewed as a liability in the eyes of many whites. How could whites and Negroes dwell together peacefully? How to rid themselves of the emancipated Negro became white America's dilemma.

2
THE NEGRO PROBLEM AND THE EMERGENCE OF EUGENICS

Let us be brought to believe it [colonization] is morally right, and, at the same time, favorable to, or, at least, not against, our interest, to transfer the African to his native clime, and we shall find a way to do it, however great the task may be. The children of Israel, to such numbers as to include four hundred thousand fighting men, went out of Egyptian bondage in a body.[1]

Speech on the Dred Scott Decision
June 26, 1867
Abraham Lincoln

What would the Negro's freedom mean for America? The thought of releasing millions of Negroes into free society struck fear in the minds of many whites for several reasons. Southern whites, for instance, feared that emancipation would cripple the Southern economy due to northern cities being "overrun" by hundreds of thousands of newly freed unskilled Negroes that had abandoned the South[2]. Northerners and Southerners alike feared that these Negroes would then be free to "mix" with whites. The validity of the fear that large numbers of Negro males would have sexual relations with white females, and the result of miscegenation (children of color), should be considered in relation to the number of castrations that were performed on African American males during the "Lynching Century."³ Many of these men were lynched based on false allegations of rape against white women. In the subconscious minds of many white males slavery, among its many functions, had served to harness the perceived sexual dominance and prowess of the Negro male. There was also fear that a "day of reckoning" would occur reminiscent of the Nat Turner Rebellion as either a consequence for the sins of whites during slavery or white's unwillingness to accept free Negroes into society as equals. The equality between blacks and whites that still evades American society today was even more inconceivable during the years leading up to and subsequent to emancipation. This was true even among whites who believed that slavery as an institution was immoral and those who believed that slavery could not survive because it was simply an unsustainable economic system. Tocqueville predicted the following outcome of slavery's abolition:

> I am obliged to confess that I do not consider the abolition of slavery as a means of delaying the struggle between the two races in the southern states. The Negroes might remain slaves for a long time without complaining; but as soon as they join the ranks of free men, they will soon be indignant at being deprived of almost all the rights of citizens; and being unable to become the equals of the whites, they will not be slow to show themselves their enemies. In the North there was every advantage in freeing the slaves; in that way one is rid of slavery without having anything to fear from the free Negroes. They were too few ever to claim their rights...⁴

Tocquevile goes on to proclaim his fears of an imminent race war:

> I confess that in considering the South I see only two alternatives for the white people living there: to free the Negroes and to mingle with them or to remain isolated from them and keep them as long as possible in slavery. Any intermediate measures seem to me likely to terminate, and that shortly, in the most horrible civil wars, and perhaps the extirpation of one or other of the two races.⁵

The French abolitionist Brissot de Warville assessed that whites "fear that if the Blacks become free they would cause trouble; on rendering them free they know not what rank to assign them in society; whether they shall establish them in separate districts or send them out of the country."[6] Before the systematic segregation of blacks and whites in the era of Jim Crow and the de facto segregation apparent today, was the idea that these two races, black and white, could *never* live in harmony. Once free, Negroes would be an economic liability on one hand and economic competitors on the other. The mere presence of the Negro was a dilemma. So how would White America deal with the problem of the Negroes presence? The most obvious solution was to send them back to the African continent from whence they were taken.

Colonization

The proposal to send free blacks back to Africa was heard as early as 1714. In a pamphlet entitled *American Defense of the Christian Golden Rule*, it was advocated that free blacks be sent back "to their own country".[7] In 1773, Samuel D. Hopkins and Ezra Stiles launched a program to train former-slaves and send them to Africa as missionaries. Hopkins, who is regarded by many as the father of colonization, believed that the following were all benefits of deportation: the opening of markets, the expansion of "civilization" and "Christianity", and social equality for blacks.[8] Funding for this program was suspended by the War of Independence several years later. Hopkins program failed due to economic cost, however the idea of deportation became quite popular among many of the religious community and others who were sympathetic to the victims of slavery. Still there were some who believed that deportation was simply in the best interest of the nation. In *Notes on the State of Virginia* Thomas Jefferson argued the following:

> Deep rooted prejudices entertained by the whites; ten thousand recollections by the blacks; the real distinctions which nature had made; and many other circumstances will divide us into parties, and produce convulsions which will probably never end but in the extermination of the one or the other race.[9]

The American Colonization Society

In 1816, John Randolph, Henry Clay, and Richard Bland Lee founded the American Colonization Society, with the initial purpose of deporting freed blacks to Africa. The society was initially the idea of Robert Finley, a Presbyterian minister. On December 21, 1816 an organizational meeting was attended by notable figures such as Henry Clay, Daniel Webster, and John Randolph. Through a series of meetings the society drafted a constitution, selected officers, and a name; they chose to call themselves the "American Society for Colonizing the Free People of Color in the United States." This was in spite of the fact that those most opposed to colonization were free blacks themselves. Indeed, there were individuals like Paul Cuffe who believed in the notion of colonization and allied with the American Colonization Society. However, many free blacks were convinced that the true intention of the American Colonization Society was to remove those whose presence threatened the social order[10]

On January 15, 1817, approximately 3,000 free blacks gathered at Bethel Church in Philadelphia in protest against the American Colonization Society.[11] James Forten, Richard Allen, Absalom Jones, And Robert Douglas, leaders of this protest who had supported Paul Cuffe, unequivocally rejected the ACS. When a branch of the society was founded in Philadelphia during the summer of 1817, hundreds of blacks protested in solidarity with their enslaved brothers and sisters. Nevertheless, there were colonization societies that were not associated with the ACS that sprouted up throughout the country. For instance, Maryland subsidized the Maryland State Colonization Society after the 1831 Nat Turner Rebellion.[12] After the Turner Rebellion, extremely oppressive laws were passed in several states to significantly restrict the lives of free blacks who many deemed largely responsible for the insurrection.[13] The Maryland State Society established its own colony which was independent of the American Colonization Society. Maryland in Liberia was largely established with public and private funds.[14] Laws were also passed, though not enforced, to forcibly extradite blacks.[15]

In 1849, Frederick Douglass professed an in issue of the North Star that, "We (Negroes) are of the opinion that the free colored people generally mean to live in America, and not in Africa; and to appropriate a large sum for removal, would merely be a waste of the public money. We do not mean to go to Liberia. Our minds are made up to live here if we can, or die here if we must; so every attempt to remove us will be, as it ought to be, labor lost."[16] However, after the Dred Scott Decision of 1857 even Douglass considered colonization in Haiti.[17]

Lincoln believed that both political parties wasted an ample opportunity to address the colonization question after the Dred Scott judgment. In a speech on the decision he declared:

> I have said that the separation of the races is the only perfect preventative of amalgamation. I have no right to say all the members of the Republican party are in favor of this, nor to say that as a party they are in favor of it. There is nothing in their platform. Such separation, if ever effected at all, must be effected by colonization; and no political party as such, is now doing anything directly for colonization. Party operations at present only favor or retard colonization incidentally…Let us be brought to believe it morally right, and, at the same time, favorable to, or, at least, not against, our interest, to transfer the African to his native clime, and we shall find a way to do it, however great the task may be. **The children of Israel, to such numbers as to include four hundred thousand fighting men, went out of Egyptian bondage in a body.**[18]

Lincoln, as did most of white America at the time, believed that Negroes and American whites were incapable of living together on equal terms. Few of his words express this notion more clearly than those spoken in 1858 when he declared:

> I am not now, nor ever haven been in favor of bringing about in any way the social or political equality of the white and black races. I am not now nor ever have been in favor or making voters or jurors of Negroes, nor of qualifying them to hold office, nor of intermarriages with white people. There is a physical difference between the white and the black races which will forever forbid the two races living together on social or political equality. There must be a position of superior and inferior and I am in favor of assigning the superior position to the white man.[19]

Throughout his presidency and up until his death, Lincoln made colonization efforts. He ordered his Secretary of State William Seward to explore the possibility of transporting large numbers of Negroes if emancipated. And, in 1861 Congress set aside $600,000 for this purpose.[20] President Lincoln believed that a warm climate like that of the Caribbean would be an ideal place for emancipated slaves. In 1863 Lincoln backed a plan that transported 450 Negroes to Ile áVache in Haiti which proved to be disastrous. Most of the settlers were decimated by starvation and smallpox.[21] In 1863 Colombia blocked a plan to send blacks to Panama. And, in the first draft of the Emancipation Proclamation Lincoln mentioned efforts to "…colonize persons of African descent, with their consent, upon this continent or elsewhere, with the previously obtained consent of the governments existing there…"[22] However, Lincoln's death by an assassin's bullet also killed much of the political will to implement colonization at the time.

Overall, colonization failed for several reasons. First, free blacks were strongly opposed to colonization. Secondly, it was simply not economically feasible to transport millions of Negroes and then sustain them for long period of times in far away countries. Finally, many countries were also unable or unwilling to accept vast numbers of blacks into their borders. The unwillingness of other countries is understandable in consideration of the friction emigration can cause within the countries where emigration occurred, as was the case in Liberia. So the question of what was to be done with the free Negro still had not been answered after the conclusion of slavery. Some believed that Negroes could not exist in a free society and would eventually become extinct.

Inevitable Extinction of the Negro Race

In the Preliminary Report on the Eighth Census published in 1862, Joseph Camp Kennedy, the statistician and superintendent of the Eighth Census, stated that the extinction of the Negro race was an "unerring certainty."[23] Kennedy believed that emancipation and integration into white society would only quicken the demise of the Negro race.[24] Kennedy's false premise was strengthened by the statistically inaccurate data of the 1870 Census. The Ninth Census of 1870 indicated that the White population increased 34.76 percent from 1860 to 1870, and the Negro population increased a mere 9.87

percent. Yet, Census reports from 1790 to 1850 show that the rate of increase among Blacks was 29.98 percent.[25] Although there were skeptics, many agreed with Kennedy's prediction of the Negro's inability to survive. The 1880 Census, however, showed an increase in birth rates among Blacks. The Negro population in 1880 was 6,577,497 while whites numbered 43,402,408. The increase from 1870 to 1880 among blacks was the largest during any decade expect 1800 to 1810. This increase gave rise to a new budding fear. E.W. Gilliam in an article in *The Popular Science Monthly* used the 1870 and 1880 Censuses to argue that if certain measures were not taken, the black population would increase at alarming rates. This increase in numbers, Gilliam argued, would result in the "Africanization" of America.[26] Nevertheless, the 1890 Census revealed a low rate of increase among Blacks, and thus solidified the notion of extinction.[27]

Insurance companies acceptance of faulty statistical analyses of the Ninth and Tenth Censuses of 1870 and 1880, pointed to the Negro's inevitable extinction. Frederick L. Hoffman a German born[28] statistician for the Prudential Insurance Company determined that "the colored race is shown to be on the downward grade."[29] He attributed this trend to seemingly higher rates of tuberculosis, sexual transmitted diseases such as syphilis and gonorrhea, and crime. Hoffman's work on the subject was published several times in the *Journal of the American Economic Association*, which gave him legitimacy. Hoffman's book *Race Traits and Tendencies of the American Negro* (1896) was also quite influential in convincing insurance companies that public expenditures for Blacks in the area of housing and healthcare be withheld due to imminent extinction. Walter F. Wilcox, Chief Statistician of the United States Census Bureau, stated "the Negroes will continue to become, as they are now becoming, a steadily smaller proportion of the population." Wilcox stated at the First Annual Conference on Race Relations of the South that the Negroes, as the Indians of this country, "will disappear before the whites, and that the remnant found capable of elevation to the level of the white man's civilization will ultimately be merged and lost in the lower classes of the whites, leaving almost no trace to mark their former existence."[30] Like Hoffman, Wilcox also attributed the inevitable demise of the Negro to criminality, crime, and vice.[31] James Vardaman referred to Wilcox's work to support the denial of suffrage and education for African Americans.[32] At this same conference, Dr. Paul Barringer, a professor of medicine at the University of Virginia, concurred that "all things point to the fact that the Negro as a race is reverting to barbarism with the inordinate criminality and degradation of the state. It seems, moreover, that he is doomed at no distant day to ultimate extinction."³³ In his book, *The American Negro: His Past and Future*, Barringer attributed the social condition of the Negro to biological inferiority, and that the race was merely reverting to its primitive state of savagery. In *The Negro in Africa and America* Joseph A. Tillangast maintained that West Africa had "no great industrial system, no science, and art could be self developed there in the first instance...The consideration of the general laws of biologic evolution would thus lead us... to believe that the mind of the lower tropical race is unfitted to assimilate the advanced civilization of a strenuous and able northern race."³⁴ He argued that the evolution in hot African climates, cannibalism, ignorance, and immorality made the Negro unable to survive in the cold climate of a civilized society. These Social Darwinist arguments and others like them led to the adoption of no policy as the best policy in matters of public health when the Negro was concerned. Why some believed that blacks in American would cease to exist after surviving the brutal system of slavery is illogical. If hundreds of years of inhumane bondage had not destroyed them, neither would the semblance of freedom that emerged with emancipation. Perhaps it was the arrogance of some whites who believed that Negroes could not exist beyond the plantation, beyond being told what to do every moment of their existence. The idea that without the force and direction of Whites the Negro would simply vanish was a vain notion. Nevertheless slavery's end marked the beginning of a new chapter in race and social relations in America.

Furthermore, the conclusion of American slavery in addition to mass migrations of Eastern Europeans in the wake of the economic crises of the 1870's and 1890's brought about the necessity for a new social theory to determine the societal status of individuals under the new rules of a transforming world.³⁵ By the time of slavery's demise, many of the accepted notions concerning diverse phenotypes had been shaped by the observations of European conquerors who had traveled throughout the "New World". During the nineteenth century, pseudo-science based on empirical data (e.g. cranial measurements) shaped European thought. Count Aurthur de Gobineau's work *Essai sur l' inégalité des races humaines* (*An Essay on the Inequality of the Human Races*) is considered one of the earliest pieces of scientific racism. In this work Gobineau separated humans into three groups (white, yellow, black). He positioned Europeans as the crown of this hierarchy and claimed that civilization only derived from contact with the white race.[36] Among whites, Gobineau placed Aryans at the top of human development and argued that "mongrelization" or "miscegenation" led to their downfall.[37]

Few scientific works of this time have been more influential on American society than Charles Darwin's *Origin of Species* (1859). In the western world it replaced the Bible as the authoritative text concerning creation and life in nature. In this book, Darwin introduced the theory of natural selection. And although it did not deal mainly with race it was presented as the justification for slavery, colonization, and racial segregation. Sir Francis Galton (1822-1911), the half-cousin of Charles Darwin, was greatly influenced by Darwin's work which made a "marked epoch on his mental development".[38] Galton used Darwin's *Origin of Species*, which was originally entitled, *Origin of Species by Means of Natural Selection, or the Preservation of Favored Races in the Struggle for Life*, to further develop his theory that the mechanisms of natural selection, which is the process by which traits become common in a population due to the effects upon the survival of the bearer, were impeded by human civilization. He argued that because many human societies protected the weak, these societies were at odds with natural selection. Without this protection the weakest members of society would be eliminated.[39] This concept was further elaborated on in *Hereditary Genius* (1869). Galton believed that certain qualities (e.g. genius and talent) in humans are hereditary. Just as artificial selection is used to exaggerate particular desirable qualities in animals, the same method could be applied to human beings. Galton wrote:

> A man's natural abilities are derived by inheritance, under exactly the same limitations as are the form and physical features of the whole organic world. Consequently, as it is easy, notwithstanding those limitations, to obtain by careful selection a permanent breed of dogs or horses gifted with peculiar powers of running, or of doing anything else, so it would be quite practicable to produce a highly gifted race of men by judicious marriages during several consecutive generations.[40]

Galton coined the term "eugenics" in his book *Inquiries into Human Faculty and Its Development* (1883). He noted the following concerning the term:

> That is, with questions bearing on what is termed in Greek, eugenes namely, good in stock, hereditary endowed with noble qualities. This, and the allied words, eugeneia, etc., are equally applicable to men, brutes, and plants. We greatly want a brief word to express the science of improving stock, which is by no means confined to questions of judicious mating, but which, especially in the case of man, takes cognizance of all influences that tend in however remote a degree to give to the more suitable races or strains of blood a better chance of prevailing speedily over the less suitable than they otherwise would have had. The word eugenics would sufficiently express the idea, it is at least a neater word and a more generalized one than viticulture which I once ventured to use.[41]

It is evident that Darwin approved of the application of his evolutionary theory concerning natural selection to human society. In a letter to H. Thiel Darwin he wrote :

> You will really believe how much interested I am in observing that you apply to moral and social questions analogous views to those which I have used in regard to the modification of species. It did not occur to me formerly that my views could be extended to such widely different and most important subjects.[42]

Darwin is well known for making the fallacious evolutionary link between ape and man in his book *On the Origin of Species by Means of Natural Selection, or the Preservation of Favored Races in the Struggle for Life*. Darwin is lesser known however, for his belief that certain races were closer than others to their ape-like ancestors. In *The Descent of a Man* (1871) Darwin predicted that the intermediary evolutionary position of the "Negro" and the baboon would lead to the extinction of them both. Darwin wrote:

> At some future period, not very distant as measured in centuries, the civilized races of man will almost certainly exterminate, and replace, the savage races throughout the world.

At the same time, the anthropomorphous apes... will no doubt be exterminated. The break will then be rendered wider, for it will intervene between man in a more civilized state, as we may hope, than the Caucasian, and some ape as low as the baboon, instead of as at present between the Negro or Australian and the Gorilla"[43]

A major flaw of Darwin's theory of evolution was that it lacked an underlying mechanism for heredity. Galton utilized statistics and classifications to address heredity and establish what was referred to as the "biometrical approach" to eugenics. Galton was concerned particularly with the transmission of traits he deemed hereditary such as intelligence, and advocated that society take the steps necessary to increase the birthrate of the "best stock". He maintained that higher birth rates could be achieved through a type of positive eugenics, which entailed state encouragement of intermarriage of the "best" men and women.[44]

Eugenics fit perfectly into an already existing framework of views concerning peoples of different races and ethnicities. Proponents of eugenics believed that through selective breeding man should directly control human evolution to encourage the reproduction of the "superior" races (i.e. Nordic & Anglo-Saxon). And some, such as Lothrop Stoddard and Madison Grant, were fearful of what they considered to be a decline in the numbers of superior stock. In his influential book *The Passing of the Great Race* (1916), Grant stated his case for the preservation of "racial purity":

> Whether we like to admit it or not, the result of the mixture of two races, in the long run, give us a race reverting to the more ancient, generalized and lower type. The cross between a white man and an Indian is an Indian; the cross between a white man and a Hindu is a Hindu; and the cross between any of the three European races and a Jew is a Jew. [45]

American Birth Control League board member and devout racist Lothrop Stoddard's work, *The Rising Tide of Color Against White World Supremacy* argued that there should be a eugenic separation between the inferior races and superior stock. Lothrop's book received praise in *Birth Control Review*.[46] Around this same time, Margaret Sanger allied with eugenicists and began opening clinics that eugenicists believed could immediately thwart the birth rates of the "unfit".

3
THE HARLEM PROJECT AND THE LEGACY OF MARGARET SANGER

Margaret Sanger is perhaps the best known birth control advocate in American history. She was instrumental in shaping U.S. policy concerning birth control through her efforts to (1) defeat Comstock laws, (2) find a sponsor to develop the "magic" birth control pill, (3) and found the American Birth Control League (Planned Parenthood). However, a lesser known fact is that Sanger was ideologically aligned with eugenicists of her day. She believed that eugenic sterilization was necessary to thwart the multiplication of certain peoples. In order to accomplish the attenuation of the Negro race Sanger formed an unlikely alliance with black leadership. The consequence of this partnership is a lasting legacy of implementing birth control measures under the guise of alleviating poverty. Sanger, who had initially focused primarily on providing birth control to Eastern European immigrant women, eventually began to concentrate on the African American population. Sanger operated an illegal abortion clinic that served impoverished immigrants in Brownsville, a section of Brooklyn, New York. But in 1919, the Birth Control Review published a "special number" concerning the need for birth control among the African American community. Around this same time, Theodore Lothrop Stoddard, published a book entitled *The Rising Tide of Color Against White World-Supremacy* (1929). In this book, Stoddard predicted the collapse of white western civilization in the wake of World War II due to the population increases among peoples of color. Stoddard, who at the time of publishing his book served on the American Birth Control League (ABCL) board of directors, received a positive review in Sanger's *Birth Control Review*.[1] A few years earlier, America's most prominent Negro scholar W.E.B. Du Bois wrote in *The Crisis*, that birth control was both science and sense applied to childbearing.[2] Dubois' endorsement of birth control perhaps prompted Sanger and the ABCL to accept speaking invitations before black audiences.[3] By 1930, Sanger successfully established a clinic in Harlem. In order to understand how Sanger was able to establish a birth control clinic in Harlem it is necessary to understand the living conditions there. When most people think of life in Harlem during the 1920's the flowering cultural movement that spanned the decade comes to mind. However, the Harlem Renaissance or the New Negro Movement as it was called at the time, occurred amidst precarious living conditions for the majority of African Americans residing in Harlem. African Americans were confined to certain areas of Harlem, which is considered by many to be the first American ghetto. During this decade, African American families in Harlem earned $1300 annually, $270 less than the typical white family.[4] In a five year study, Dr. Winifred Nathan found that deaths from tuberculosis in Harlem, due to poor sanitation, overcrowding, substandard nutrition and overall living conditions were substantially higher than the rest of New York City.[5] Harlem death rates from tuberculosis were 193 per 100,000 compared to 81 per 100,000 for all of New York City.[6] In fact, the instances of death resulting from tuberculosis were so high that the Harlem Tuberculosis and Health Committee, a branch of the New York Tuberculosis and Health Association, was founded during the 1920's. Between 1923 and 1927 the African American infant mortality rate was 111 per 1,000, compared to 64.5 per 1,000 for all of New York City.[7]

On November 21, 1930 the American Birth Control League opened an experimental clinic in Harlem. Earlier in the month, Sanger maintained that the clinic would be founded for the "benefit of the colored people".[8] Segregation, high unemployment, high infant mortality rate, and disproportionate deaths from tuberculosis were all reasons provided by the ABCL to justify its efforts in Harlem. Largely due to the harsh realities of Harlem's black population, Sanger was able to convince some of Harlem's most prominent blacks to form an advisory council for the Harlem Clinic. She was even invited to speak at Abyssinian Baptist Church, the largest black church in Harlem. Although prominent blacks were advocating birth control, the masses of blacks in Harlem still grappled with it as a method to improve their lives. Ironically, the Harlem Clinic was largely financed through private donations, one of which being the Julius Rosenwald Fund. The Julius Rosenwald Fund in conjunction with the Public Health Service (PHS) sponsored the Tuskegee Syphilis Experiment in Macon County Alabama in 1932.[9] The Tuskegee Experiment is arguably the most infamous biomedical experiment in U.S. history. This seroprevalance study, just like the Harlem Clinic, was characterized to benefit the overall health of rural African Americans who were believed to suffer from high rates of syphilis.

Persistently, Sanger continued to target the Black community with eugenic birth control. In 1932, a special issue of *Birth Control Review* entitled "The Negro Number" was published specifically for African Americans. Again, black leaders of prominence were recruited. This time it was to write articles in favor of birth control. In this issue Du Bois argued that the majority of "ignorant" Negroes bred in a way that was imprudent and disastrous. According to Du Bois, the increase in the Negro birth rate was largely from those individuals within the Negro population who were the least intelligent and the least fit to raise children properly.[10] Du Bois was one of several prominent African American scholars who wholly supported Sanger's eugenic plan to limit the births of impoverished blacks. So why did prominent African Americans support the negative eugenic program to limit black births? The black elite did not necessarily believe in the inherent inferiority of the black race as a whole. Rather, many of them reasoned that poverty could be alleviated if Blacks simply had fewer children. Fewer children, in their estimation, would mean fewer expenses, an increase in educational opportunities, and the achievement of the overall objective to integrate into the larger white society. This was contrary to much of the thinking of working class blacks who were more influenced by religious convictions. Du Bois believed that the resistance that existed in the Negro community to birth control was a conflict of ideals between Negroes that desired to improve their economic state of affairs and Negroes, who because of their religious faith, believed that birth control was a sin.[11] Thus Du Bois encouraged Sanger to use a religious appeal to transform many blacks thinking regarding birth control. He believed that African Americans were receptive to "intelligent propaganda of any sort."[12]

Sanger agreed with Du Bois' suggestion and in a December 19, 1939 letter to Dr. Clarence Gamble wrote that a religious appeal was the most effective approach to convince the black masses to accept birth control, and that ministers would be able to thwart objections from blacks who protested extermination of the Negro population.[13] In 1939 Sanger created the Negro Project and maintained that it was established to assist poor colored people.[14] It is critical to point out Sanger's success in recruiting some of the most prominent leaders of the black community to serve on the Birth Control Federation of America's National Advisory Council, because it is quite unlikely that Sanger could have been as successful in her program to reduce black numbers without the compliance of exceptional figures such as Mary McLeod Bethune, Charles S. Johnson, Claude A. Bennett, Arthur Spingarn, Eugene Kinckle Jones, Adam Clayton Powell Jr., E. Franklin Frazier, and of course W.E.B. Du Bois.

However, to profess that Sanger was able to bamboozle the "best" and the "brightest" Negroes of her time into accepting negative eugenics against their own race is not entirely accurate. Black leaders and intellectuals understood that there were individuals who did not have the best interests of the Negro race at heart. They were also acquainted with the horrendous condition of the black masses. For example, during Du Bois' time in the South he became acquainted with the vast poverty of his people and the violence they suffered through lynching. Adam Clayton Powell understood and fought for better housing conditions for black tenants in Harlem. Black leaders were conscious of the fact that extreme segregation and racism had confined blacks into a state of abject poverty. There seemed to be very few opportunities for educated blacks and none for the masses of Negroes. Birth control was viewed merely as a way to limit the extreme poverty that plagued African Americans in spite of the malicious intentions of racist eugenicists. Black intellectuals W.E.B. Du Bois, Charles S. Johnson and E. Franklin Frazier contended that the black condition was not due to inferior biological traits but rather a consequence of extreme forms of racism. For instance, in 1927 Du Bois debated the "father" of Nordic supremacy Lothrop Stoddard concerning scientific racism. Also, unlike racist eugenicists, black leaders were not proponents of compulsory sterilization that eventually occurred disproportionately among blacks. But, the black intellectuals greatest failure was their disregard for the moral implications of their actions. The oppressed, the exploited, the powerless must always consider the ethical implications of the strategies they implement in the quest for liberation. The consequence of the egregious moral failure of black leadership in this critical time of black advancement is the lasting legacy of birth control use and currently abortion to suppress the black population in order to alleviate the social problems within the black community.

Charles Darwin (1809-1882)
Naturalist
Founder of evolutionary biology through natural selection
Author of *On the Origin of Species by Means of Natural Selection, or the Preservation of Favoured Races in the Struggle for Life*, 1859

Francis Galton (1822-1911)
Cousin of Charles Darwin
Author of *Hereditary Genius*, 1869

Madison Grant (1865-1937)
Eugenicist
Author of *The Passing of the Great Race*, 1916

Lothrop Stoddard (1883-1950)
Eugenicist
Author of *The Rising Tide of Color Against White World-Supremacy*, 1920

Oliver Wendell Holmes Jr. (1841-1935)
Associate Justice of the United States Supreme Court
In Office (1902-1932)

Margaret Higgins Sanger (1879-1966)
Founder of American Birth Control League, which became Planned Parenthood
Birthed the Harlem Project

W.E.B. Du Bois (1868-1963)
Scholar, Sociologist, Pan Africanist
Advisor to Margaret Sanger

Charles S. Johnson (1893-1956)
Sociologist
First Black President of Fisk University

Julius Rosenwald (1862-1932)
Business Executive
Philanthropist
Established the Rosenwald Fund in 1917. The Rosenwald Fund sponsored the Tuskegee Syphilis Experiment and funded the Harlem Clinic.

Test subjects from the Tuskegee Syphilis Study. The Tuskegee Syphilis Study lasted from 1932 to 1972.

Karl Gunnar Mydral (1898-1987)
Swedish Economist
Author of *An American Dilemma: The Negro Problem and Modern Democracy*, 1944

4
THE RHINELAND "BASTARDES"

Toward the end of the 19th century, the notion of racial hygiene became a major concern in Germany for several reasons. Industrialization, mass migrations, and urbanization resulted in overcrowded impoverished cities that were crime ridden and full of disease. More individuals were also being diagnosed as mentally retarded. Furthermore, many health professionals held that the birthrate was declining while "degeneration" among the German population was increasing. At the same time, there were discoveries in the areas of bacteriology and genetics that promised to address the nation's problems. In the area of bacteriology August Weismann presented the germ-plasm theory of heredity in Das Keimplasma (1829) which contradicted Lamarck's theory of acquired characteristics. Weismann argued that preceding generations were unable to inherit acquired characteristics. For degeneration theorists Weismann's findings suggested that the environment could not positively foster improvements in the social condition.

The Deutsche Gesellschaft für Rassenhygiene (German Society for Racial Hygiene), established on June 22, 1905 by Alfred Ploetz, dedicated its first issue, *Archiv für Rassen- und Geesellscaftsbiologie* (Journal of Racial and Social Biology), to Weismann and named him honorary chairman of the organization.[1] Ploetz who coined the term Rassenhygiene (racial hygiene) believed that selective production and sterilization were both necessary to regain the "purity" of the Nordic stock.[2] Among the first leaders of the organization were several of

Weismann's students such as renowned geneticists Fritz Lenz and Eugen Fischer[3]. Fischer, a professor of anthropology, medicine, and eugenics, was instrumental in the development of theories of racial hygiene that justified the extermination and compulsory sterilization of thousands of victims. In 1908 he received a grant to conduct field research concerning the physical and psychological traits of the children of white male settlers (German or Boar) and black women (Hottentots) in German Southwest Africa colonies (current day Namibia). Fischer conducted a study of 310 children who were the offspring of Boers and Hottentots.[4] For the purpose of determining racial dominance, these children known as "Rehoboth bastards" were subjected to demeaning examinations (e.g. head and measurements, hair and skin examinations, etc.). Fischer concluded that the "mischlinge" (cross-breed) should be exterminated after their usefulness for Germany came to an end. Based on the findings of Fischer by 1912, intermarriage in German colonies was restricted. After the German defeat in World War I people of mixed heritage became the target of racial hygienists. Under the terms of the Treaty of Versailles, Germany lost its African colonies and was forced to endure Allied French occupation of the Rhineland. For many years the Germans had bitterly contested with the French over the Rhineland. And many racists, including Nazis, were infuriated by the presence of Africans among the French colonial troops. Hitler considered France to be the bitter enemy of Germany, an enemy that intentionally introduced men of African descent into the Rhineland as an act of vengeance.

German officials attempted to garner international support to counter the Treaty of Versailles by framing the presence of African troops in the Rhineland as an attempt by the French to compromise the racial integrity of Germany. Soon, rumors of rape by the African troops spread throughout the Rhineland.[5] The truth was simply that hundreds of German women produced offspring within the confines of marriage or consensual sexual relations with African troops. The estimated 500-600 children conceived through these unions were referred to as half breeds, mulattos, or most commonly as the "Rheinlandbastardes" (Rhineland bastards). Their presence meant the "contamination" of German blood. It was also realized quite early that the existence of these children and their likely progeny was an unacceptable perpetual reminder of defeat in World War I.

During the 1920's there were several attempts to number the so called Rhineland Bastards. Between 1923 and 1927 approximately half of these 600 or so children were identified. However these identifications relied solely upon voluntary statements by parents who were usually less than willing to comply with this census due to the racist nature of the surveys. Calls by the Palatine Commisar and Privy Councilor of the Bavarian Interior in 1927 to thwart the danger of the "black scourge" through compulsory immigration or sterilization were rejected by the Wiemar Republic. Although the Weimar regime was racist, laws concerning compulsory sterilization programs to foster racial purity were considered politically imprudent. However, with the rise of the National Socialist Party in 1933 eugenics became central to government policy.

In 1933 Herman Göring, Prussian minister of the interior ordered that data be gathered on the "Rhineland bastards" in various cities. In the same year, Dr. Hans Macco published a pamphlet entitled, *Racial Problems in the Third Reich* which called for the sterilization of children of "mixed descent". Macco maintained that Rhineland children of mixed descent were conceived through rape or prostitution. Hans argued without compulsory sterilization racial deterioration would be felt for centuries to come.[6]

On January 1, 1934 The Law for the Protection of Hereditary Health: The Attempt to Improve German Aryan Breed law went into effect. According to this law doctors had to report individuals that were deemed unfit to the Hereditary Health Courts. It should be noted that the plan of compulsory sterilization was modeled largely on the 1922 California Sterilization Law. Under this law the number of Blacks sterilized was twofold that of whites. Just as the California Law the Nazi sterilization laws did not justify sterilization solely on the grounds of race (e.g. feeble-mindedness).

By 1935, Division II of the Expert Committee for Population and Racial Policy determined that the children of the Rhineland should be discretely sterilized. To circumvent the 1933 Sterilization law, parent "consent" was a requirement prior to sterilization. In 1937, Hitler secretly ordered the sterilization of the "Rheinlandbastardes". In the same year, Special Commission No. 3, whose members included Eugen Fischer, was formed to achieve this goal. Data was gathered concerning youths of "mixed" background from various institutions (e.g. churches, schools, etc.). This information was used to locate children who were then taken from their homes, schools, of off of the street and brought before a commission. In practically every case the commission ruled in favor of sterilization. After the ruling the child was immediately taken to be sterilized. Of the estimated 500-800 children who were sterilized between 1935 and 1937, many had no representation, or parents who were coerced into signing "parental consent" by the Gestapo. Victims of these commissions were required to carry sterilization certificates. Hans Hauck, an Afro German who was sterilized in the mid 1930's, stated that the procedure occurred without anesthetic.[7] It is extremely difficult to account for all of the sterilizations of Blacks during the Nazi regime because of their illegality. What is certain is the influence of American eugenics on the Nazi sterilization program. During the Nuremberg trials over forty Nazi doctors credited American eugenicists with providing the ideological framework for their program of extermination.[8] In their defense Nazi eugenicists quoted Supreme Court Justice Oliver Wendell Holmes who wanted to inhibit "those who are manifestly unfit from continuing their kind".[9] Hitler not only studied American eugenics, but in a letter to Madison Grant referred to Grant's book *The Passing of the Great Race* as his "bible"[10]. Strong ties also existed between German eugenicists and eugenicists from the Carnegie Institution. Pointing out seemingly American hypocrisy was not a trivial argument. C.M. Geothe, a leading eugenicist, visited Germany and was convinced that German eugenicists had been tremendously influenced by American thought.[11]

Law for the Protection of Hereditary Health: The Attempt to Improve the German Aryan Breed (July 14, 1933)

Article I.
Anyone who suffers from an inheritable disease may be surgically sterilized if, in the judgment of medical science, it could be expected that his descendants will suffer from serious inherited mental or physical defects. Anyone who suffers from one of the following is to be regarded as inheritably diseased within the meaning of this law:
    Congenital feeble-mindedness
    Schizophrenia
    Manic-depression
    Congenital epilepsy
    hereditary blindness
    hereditary deafness
    serious inheritable malformations

Article II.
Anyone who requests sterilization is entitled to it. If he be incapacitated or under a guardian because of low state of mental health or not yet 18 years of age, his legal guardian is empowered to make the request. In other cases of limited capacity the request must receive the approval of the legal representative. If a person be of age and has a nurse, the latter's consent is required.

The request must be accompanied by a certificate from a citizen who is accredited by the German Reich stating that the person to be sterilized has been informed about the nature and consequence of sterilization.

The request for sterilization can be recalled.

Article III.
Sterilization may also be recommended by:
The official physician
The official in charge of a hospital, sanitarium, or prison.

Article IV.
The request for sterilization must be presented in writing to, or placed in writing by the office of the Health Inheritance Court. The statement concerning the request must be certified by a medical document or authenticated in some other way. The business office of the court must notify the official physician.

Article VII. The proceedings of the Health Inheritance Court are secret.

Article X. The Supreme Health Insurance Court retains final jurisdiction.

5
THE MISSISSIPPI APPENDECTOMY

When most Americans think of compulsory sterilizations, images of Nazi Germany under the reign of Hitler come to mind. However, compulsory sterilization was not uncommon in the United States. It is a fact that the sterilization laws of Germany were largely patterned after American sterilization laws.[12] Forced sterilization in America was initially used against white populations deemed "unfit to breed". This chapter explains how compulsory sterilization came to be largely used against African Americans.

Buck v. Bell

The state of Indiana passed the first eugenic involuntary sterilization law in 1907. However, this law was legally flawed. To address this defect, Harry Laughlin of the Eugenics Record Office at the Cold Springs Laboratory created a model sterilization law and had it reviewed by legal experts so that it would be upheld in court. He found that due to the possible legal ramifications many doctors were reluctant to perform sterilizations. In 1924, the Commonwealth of Virginia passed a statute that was largely based on Haughlin's model. To test this statute, Superintendent of the Virginia State Colony for Epileptics and Feeble Minded Dr. Albert Sidney Priddy filed a petition to sterilize a young women named Carrie Buck. Carrie Buck was an 18 year old patient that had given birth to an illegitimate child. She had been deemed feeble-minded and was committed to the Virginia State Colony by her adoptive parents. It was learned later that Carrie was impregnated by the nephew of her adoptive parents who raped her. It is likely that her parents had her committed for feeblemindedness to protect the family name. Dr. Piddy claimed that Buck had the mental age of a nine year old and was a genetic threat to society. According to Piddy, Carrie Buck's mother had the mental age of an eight year old and had a record of prostitution an immorality. Although Carrie Buck had reached the sixth grade, Piddy maintained that she was "incorrigible" and should be sterilized. In an 8 to 1 decision the Supreme Court ruled that the sterilization law was constitutional. Justice Oliver Wendell Holmes wrote the following in the Court's ruling:

> We have seen more than once that the public welfare may call upon the best citizens for their lives. It would be strange if it could not call upon those who already sap the strength of the State for these lesser sacrifices, often not felt to be such by those concerned, to prevent our being swamped with incompetence. It is better for all the world, if instead of waiting to execute degenerate offspring for crime, or let them starve for their imbecility, society can prevent those who are manifestly unfit from continuing their kind. Their principle that sustains compulsory vaccination is broad enough to cover cutting the Fallopian tubes…Three generations of imbeciles are enough.[13]

Buck v. Bell legitimated compulsory sterilization and as a result states that had sterilization laws on the books began to enforce them more often. Over twenty states added new sterilization legislation or revised existing statutes similar to the Virginia statute. During the decade following Buck v. Bell impoverished whites such as Carrie Buck were the primary targets of sterilization. However, by the 1950's compulsory sterilization of Blacks, especially of those living in South states, became commonplace.

Alabama

In 1919 Alabama passed sterilization legislation that gave the superintendent of the Alabama Home for the Feebleminded the authority to sterilize any inmate if the Alabama Insane Hospitals superintendent agreed. Around 1923, both positions were merged into one and a eugenicist named Dr. William D. Partlow held sole authority over who would be sterilized. Between 1919 and 1935, Partlow sterilized every patient (224 individuals) that was discharged from facilities under his control. The sterilization law in Germany was the inspiration for Alabama to expand its own sterilization laws. The State Public Health Officer, Dr. James Norment Baker stated in 1934 that "the whole civilized world will watch, with keen interest, the bold experiment just launched by Germany in mass sterilization,". He was convinced that Germany would save a substantial amount of money. Baker influenced the legislature to expand Alabama's short reaching sterilization law into the largest in the nation. Under this legislation, the following individuals were subject to sterilization: individuals committed to insane and feebleminded facilities, homosexuals, convicted rapists, sadists, masochists, and sodomists. The legislation also allowed for the sterilization of any individual that was "habitually and constantly dependent upon public relief or support by charity." Legislation directed at those dependent upon state welfare led to the sterilization of impoverished blacks in Alabama for decades.

A 1973 case involving two teenage girls from Montgomery, Alabama, who became the victims of sterilization abuse, brought national attention to compulsory sterilization in the state. Mary Alice Relf (age 14) and Minnie Relf (age 12) were the youngest of six children born to parents on public assistance. The federally funded Montgomery Community Action Agency requested permission from Mrs. Relf to inject Depo-Provera into her young girls. Mrs. Relf, who had received little formal education, signed the consent form with an "X". It should be noted that months prior to the Montgomery Community Action Agency's request, the federal government had ordered that such injections end due to the carcinogenic effect they induced in test animals. It was later learned that although Mrs. Relf had consented to a temporary birth control procedure, her daughters had been permanently sterilized. The Relfs, with the help of the Southern Poverty Law Center, filed a class action lawsuit which helped to expose the widespread sterilization abuse of poor African American women.[14] The district court found that large numbers of welfare recipients were coerced into being sterilized in order to avoid termination of their welfare benefits. It was also discovered that federally funded programs had sterilized between 100,000 to 150,000 poor women, the majority of whom were black.[15] Not only did this case lead to more awareness of this unethical practice, but it also lead to stricter regulations of federal funding for sterilizations.

South Carolina

Welfare beneficiaries in South Carolina were also targeted for sterilization. Marietta Williams of Aiken County, a 20 year old mother of two, agreed to sterilization after her third baby was delivered. Williams received welfare benefits and the only obstetrician that accepted Medicaid was Dr. Clovis Pierce. Dr. Pierce refused to deliver her third child unless she agreed to undergo sterilization. Pierce told Dorothy Waters when she refused to undergo the procedure, "Listen here, young lady, this is my tax money paying for this baby and I'm tired of paying for illegitimate children. If you don't want this sterilization, find another doctor." In a period of 18 months prior to 1972, Pierce received $60,000 of taxpayer's money in Medicaid fees. In 1972, out of thirty-four deliveries that were paid for through Medicaid, eighteen of these women underwent sterilization. All of these sterilizations were performed on African American women by Dr. Clovis Pierce. Pierce later stated that it was his policy to sterilize mothers who received welfare benefits after their third baby in order to reduce welfare rolls.

North Carolina

In 1965, Nial Cox underwent sterilization. Cox who lived with her mother and siblings became pregnant by her boyfriend at the age of 18. Nial did not receive welfare directly; however, her mother Devora collected welfare benefits for herself, Nial and all of her other children. Once Nial's pregnancy was discovered by a social worker it was insisted that Nial be sterilized. If Nial's mother had refused, she and her children would have lost the main source of income for herself as well as for her children. Confronted with the threat of losing the income that sustained her entire family Nial's mother conceded. The North Carolina Eugenics Board was petitioned to have Cox sterilized. Through a North Carolina law that allowed for the sterilization of individuals with mental defects, Cox was permanently sterilized. Cox was labeled "feeble-minded" despite the fact that there was no evidence of her having any mental defect.

A similar fate happened to Elaine Riddick Jesse, born Elaine Riddick, of Winfall, North Carolina. At the age of 13 she became pregnant after being sexually assaulted by a man in his 20's. Riddick's assailant threatened her with death if she did not agree to keep quite about the assault. Once the pregnancy was discovered by a Perquimans County social worker, Riddick's grandmother was pressured to sign a consent form to have Elaine sterilized. If she had refused Elaine would have been sent to live in an orphanage. Riddick's parents were unable to care for her and she and one sibling lived with their grandmother while five of her other siblings were already living in an orphanage. Woodard was illiterate and more than likely unwittingly signed the consent form with an "X". Consent for sterilizations was often viewed as a nuisance rather than an ethical obligation by many social workers. Elaine's report read as follows: Report 8. Deloris Elaine -(N)- Perquimans County Social information: Age 13. Single. Pregnant. Psychological April 5, 1967. MA9-6: IQ75

This thirteen year old girl expects her first child in March 1968…She has never done any work and gets along so poorly with others that her school experience was poor. Because of Elaine's inability to control herself, and her promiscuity- there are community reports of her "running around" and out late at night unchaperoned, the physician has advised sterilization… This will at least prevent additional children from being born to this child who cannot care for herself, and can never function in any way as a parent. Diagnosis: Feebleminded. Notwithstanding the unethical practice of compulsory sterilization, this diagnosis is problematic for several reasons. First, Elaine's environment and the impact that it may have had on her intelligence was not taken into consideration. In addition, the score on IQ tests that would deem someone as "feebleminded" and a candidate for sterilization was 70. According to the Board's summary, Riddick was labeled "feebleminded" despite the fact that she scored a 75. The young mother to be entered Chowan Hospital in Edenton to deliver her son and without her knowledge or consent was sterilized. In 1973, after Jessie and her husband could not conceive she learned of what had been done to her. Between 1929 and 1974 the North Carolina Eugenics Board sterilized over 7,600 individuals. Initially, more whites were sterilized than blacks. Between 1933 and 1974 the North Carolina Eugenics Board ordered the sterilization of approximately 2,000 boys and girls some of who were as young as 10 years old. And, by the mid-60's approximately 60% of women that underwent sterilization were African American.

In 2005, House Bill 1607 was filed which called for $69 million in compensation for sterilization victims like Elaine Riddick.

Mississippi

In 1964, amidst oppressive legislation to respond to Freedom marches in Mississippi lawmakers introduced House Bill 180. In its original form, HB 180 allowed for the incarceration of parents who had their second child out of wedlock. This prison term could be avoided if the mother agreed to sterilization. In response, the Student Nonviolent Coordinating Committee (SNCC) issued a pamphlet entitled "Genocide in Mississippi". The efforts of SNCC were instrumental in raising awareness of the eugenic law.[16] Soon newspapers throughout the country carried the news of compulsory sterilizations and the Mississippi legislature was forced to backpedal on its initial objective although a watered down version of the bill was passed. Nevertheless, poor black females were still vulnerable to involuntary sterilization.

Fanie Lou Hamer, delegate for the Mississippi Freedom Democratic Party and civil rights activist, was also a victim of involuntary sterilization. In 1961, Hamer checked into the hospital to have a uterine tumor removed. Unbeknownst to her, the doctor had removed her uterus. In 1965, before a crowd in Washington, D.C. Hamer claimed that in her hometown of Sunflower County, Mississippi, 60% of black women have been subjugated to postpartum sterilization without their consent. In fact, hysterectomies were so common in Mississippi that doctors referred to the procedure as the "Mississippi Appendectomy". The injustice that was committed against Hamer was the impetus behind her political involvement.

Northern Cities

Involuntary sterilizations were also occurring in the north as well. In April of 1972, the Boston Globe ran a front page story about a complaint filed by Boston City Hospital students who claimed that needless hysterectomies were being performed on poor African American patients.[17] In 1973, the Public Citizen Health Research released a report of detailed conversations at several medical teaching facilities- Boston City Hospital, Los Angeles County Hospital, and Baltimore City Hospital.[18] In many of these conversations, doctors admitted to coercing women into unnecessary hysterectomies for the purpose of practice. One Boston City Hospital resident expressed the desire to perform hysterectomies instead of tubal ligations which in his estimation could be performed by a trained primate. According to this report, approximately 70% of about 80 hospitals had violated 1974 sterilization consent regulations. Due to a lack of adequate recordkeeping and falsified records it is impossible to know just how many African American women were forcibly sterilized nation-wide.

ELISHA J. ISRAEL

Fannie Lou Hamer (1917-1977)
Civil Rights Leader

6
TEENS, "WELFARE QUEENS", AND "CRACK MOMMAS" NEED BIRTH CONTROL!

Well into the 1970's, African American women were involuntary or unnecessarily sterilized at the hands of medical professionals. For instance, research from a fertilization study conducted in 1970 revealed that 20% of African American married women had been sterilized.[1] However, in recent years, efforts to curb the black birth rate have been achieved more subtly through the use of long-term contraceptives. The use of contraceptives such as Norplant and Depo-Provera have been championed by educators, legislators, and judges to significantly reduce the numbers of children born to black teens, black welfare recipients, and black women facing incarceration. The rationale for targeting these specific populations is identical to the underlying principle which was the impetus for the Harlem Project. Simply put, impoverishment warrants sterilization. This logic resonates with much of the larger white society, many of whom have accepted the racialized framing of African American women as promiscuous women who procreate uncontrollably with multiple "baby daddies". It is true that children being born out of wedlock is an alarming trend within the African American community. However, the stereotypical labeling of the vast majority of black women or all poor black women as overly sexualized partially explains why long-term contraceptives have been so successfully aimed at black females often under circumstances that would be deemed unacceptable or unethical if under these same circumstances the females were white.

Norplant

Norplant was developed by the Population Council and distributed by Wyeth-Ayerst Laboratories, a division of Home Products Corporation. In 1990 Progestin levonorgestrel (Norplant), a form of the female hormone progesterone, emerged as a long-term contraceptive. The Norplant Contraceptive System entails surgically implanting six rods into the upper arm. These rods dispense levonorgestrel over the course of five years. Norplant causes cervical mucus to thicken which blocks sperm which prevents conception. Immediately after FDA approval the African American female population was targeted.

In a Philadelphia Inquirer Editorial entitled "Poverty and Norplant: Can Contraception Reduce the Underclass?" Donald Kimelman argued that the root of poverty was the prevalence of pregnancies among blacks who were economically the least able to take care of children.[2] In this editorial, which was published two days after the FDA approved the usage of Norplant, Kimelman suggested that financial incentives be given to female welfare recipients who agree to use the contraceptive. Without subsidy, the initial high cost of Norplant ($365 for the capsules, $100-$500 for procedure, and $150-$500 for removal) made it out of reach for many poor women of color. Legislators across the country also agreed that Norplant could reduce the rates of reproduction among poor African American women on public assistance. By reducing the number of welfare recipients in this manner, legislators could significantly reduce their welfare budgets. Politicians around the country surmised that female welfare recipients should be "encouraged" to utilize these contraceptives and through legislation took the necessary steps to, as Kimelman had suggested, reduce the underclass. For instance, a 1991 Kansas bill was introduced that would mandate a $500 grant to welfare recipients who agreed to use Norplant, and $50 each year the implant was maintained.[3] Similar bills were proposed in Tennessee, and Washington state.[4][5] Also in 1991, Louisiana state representative and former Grand Wizard of the Ku Klux Klan, David Duke, presented legislation that proposed paying women on welfare $100 annually to use Norplant.⁶ In Mississippi, a bill was introduced that would make welfare for women with four or more children contingent upon an agreement to use Norplant. In Ohio a welfare mother could receive a one time payment of $1,000 and an increase of monthly cash assistance by 150% if she agreed to be *permanently* sterilized.⁷ Those who were willing to use Depo-Provera or Norplant could expect to receive a one time payment of $500 and a 10% increase in subsidy every six months not exceeding the 150% level. In addition, under this legislation welfare mothers would have to identify the father of their children to the state. Identified men had the following options:

1) Pay child support

2) Perform community service

3) Receive $1,000 to be sterilized

4) Serve two years in prison.

In 1993, Tennessee notified all public assistance recipients in writing of the "opportunity" to receive Norplant free of charge. Eventually all fifty states, including Washington D.C. provided financing for Norplant insertions through Medicaid. Many black women on Medicaid who wanted the Norplant insertion removed due to side effects found it difficult. Often Medicaid recipients were not informed that they would have to pay for Norplant removal themselves. One survey found that women who had the contraceptive inserted immediately after child birth were not reimbursed by Medicaid if complaints of side effects occurred after the 60-day postpartum Medicaid eligibility period.⁸

Norplant and African American Teens

When Norplant was first distributed in 1991-1992 Black teenage girls were primary targets. The rate of teenage pregnancy was used as justification to introduce the contraceptive to this population. This was done despite the fact that at the time teen pregnancy was in overall decline with the highest rate of decline being among black teenage girls.[9] However, the teenage pregnancy rate in Baltimore was much higher than the national average. This made Baltimore a prime site to introduce the contraceptive. Throughout the city, health providers encouraged African American teens to have the device implanted into their arms. School clinics were also utilized to offer teenage girls Norplant with or without parental consent. One such school, Laurence G. Paquin Middle School, a middle school in Baltimore for pregnant teens or teens that already have children, launched the first pilot program for Norplant implantation. At the time of the pilot program, of the 350 girls who attended the school 345 were black. In her book, *Medical Apartheid: The Dark History of Medical Experimentation on Black Americans from Colonial Times to the Present*, Harriet Washington maintains that the Population Council used data concerning health effects of Norplant usage to conduct a large scale experiment.[10]

The "Option" for Women Facing Incarceration

Norplant was also presented as an "option" for women who were facing incarceration. Norplant was utilized as a tool to reduce the "underclass" by making coercive sterilization a condition of probation and lesser prison sentences for women deemed unworthy of motherhood or unable to be good mothers. In 1991, less than a month after FDA approval of Norplant, California Superior Court Judge Howard Broadman gave Darlene Johnson, who pled guilty to three counts of felony child abuse, the "choice" between seven years in prison or a one year sentence and three years probation. The lighter sentence was contingent on Johnson's willingness to have Norplant inserted into her arm. When Johnson inquired of the drug's safety, Judge Broadman assured her that it was safe and that any adverse effects could be reversed by simple removal. Johnson, who was eight months pregnant, had no lawyer present at the time, and with no medical consultation agreed. However, not long after, Johnson learned that Norplant was contraindicated in individuals such as herself who suffered from diabetes and hypertension. With the assistance of the American Civil Liberties Union appealed Broadman's order on the grounds that it was unconstitutional. Even The California attorney general wrote a brief in which he argued that

Judge Broadman's order should be rescinded because it was coercive and the defendant was uniformed. Nevertheless, Judge Broadman denied her motion and found that Johnson had given informed consent. Eventually, Johnson's appeal was deemed moot and dismissed after she violated her probation by testing positive for drug use. This was not an isolated occurrence. Soon after FDA approval of Norplant, many women who were convicted on charges of drug abuse or child abuse faced the "option" of a fertile lengthy stint behind bars or a sterile reduced sentence. Some may argue that this policy of proposing sterilization instead of long term incarceration affects races impartially. However, African American women are more likely to come in contact with government officials (i.e. welfare) and consequentially more prone to be reported for child abuse than white women. Secondly, African American women have been largely stereotyped as poor mothers thus making it more acceptable for these women to be coerced into temporary sterilization.

Depo-Provera "aka" "The Shot"

Depo-Provera, "depo", or "the shot" is a hormonal contraceptive. Depo is administered in the form of an injection in the arm or buttocks every three months. It thwarts pregnancy by suppressing ovulation and makes cervical mucus uninhabitable for sperm. Depo-Provera has had a long and controversial history. For over a decade (1967-1978) the largest known human experiment on the effects of Depo-Provera was conducted through the Grady Memorial Family Planning Clinic in Atlanta, Georgia. A vast majority of these subjects were African American women who were receiving public assistance. In violation of Food and Drug Administration (FDA) regulations, trials were conducted without the consent and knowledge of the participants. In 1978 investigators sent to Grady Clinic discovered that many of those who had given consent were not informed of the possible side effects. Also, during the experiment, Depo-Provera was administered to women whose medical conditions indicated that doing so would significantly endanger their health. Several of the women in the study developed cancer and severe depression. During the trials, deaths caused by cancer and suicide were not reported to the FDA as is required. Record keeping was questionable to say the least. Over half of the 13,000 women were not available for follow-studies. It is important to note that in 1967, Upjohn, the manufacturer of Depo-Provera at the time, submitted a New Drug Application which should not have been considered based on new application guidelines that were passed the same year. The application should not have been considered prior to the results from the animal studies. Nevertheless, the beagle and monkey tests began a year *after* the large-scale human clinical trial at Grady.

The beagle and rhesus monkey tests initiated in 1968 linked Depo-Provera with breast and uterine cancer. By 1973, reports on the beagles study revealed elevated rates of breast tumors. This sparked a debate in the scientific community over whether beagles were overly sensitive to artificial progesterone. Of course Upjohn argued that beagles were not appropriate test subjects due to their hypersensitivity. However, Dr. Solomon Sobel of the FDA testified of the fact that there were no contraceptives that were carcinogenic in beagles on the American market. In 1978, Commissioner Donald Kennedy denied Upjohn's application for Depo-Provera use as a contraceptive. Kennedy refused for the following reasons:

1.) Beagle studies revealed high rates of breast cancer
2.) Increased risks of birth defects in human fetuses that were exposed to the drug
3.) Significant population in need of the drug had not yet been determined

Upjohn appealed to the FDA Public Board of Inquiry. The board replied, "Never has a drug whose target population is entirely healthy people been shown to be so pervasively carcinogenic in animals as has Depo-Provera."[11] However, two significant events led to the contraceptives approval. In 1987, the FDA began using rats and mice in cancer testing instead of beagles and monkeys; Depo-Provera did not cause cancer in rats or mice. And in 1991, the World Health Organization (WHO) reported that there was no "evidence for increased risk of breast cancer with long duration of use." This decision was based on a nine-year study in three countries. It should be noted that the long duration of use study was conducted by Upjohn. Finally, in 1992 Depo-Provera was approved by the FDA. In a very short time Depo-Provera was predominately used by African American women. A 1994 study found that 84% of Depo-Provera users were African American and 74% were low income.

African American women are still largely targeted for Depo-Provera and are twice as likely to use the contraceptive as their white counterparts.[12]

These dangerous contraceptives have been pushed, often aggressively, to African American women by health providers despite the health disparities within the black community. Both Norplant and Depo-Provera have been shown to be contraindicated in women who suffer from health conditions which are found at higher rates among black women (e.g. blood clots, hypertension, heart disease, diabetes, breast cancer, obesity, and depression).[13] Many women in general, however, suffered side effects so severe from Norplant use that by 1996 over 50,000 lawsuits and 70 class actions were filed against Wyeth, its subsidiaries, and doctors. Wyeth was able to ward off lawsuits initially, but it did offer out-of-court cash settlements of $1,500 to approximately 36,000 who maintained that they had not been properly warned about the severe side-effects of Norplant usage. In 2000 Wyeth halted Norplant distribution in the U.S. Depo-Provera, on the other hand is still on the market. In addition to side effects such as hair loss, acne, rashes, menstrual irregularity, bone loss, weight gain, and depression, Depo-Provera use may increase the risk of sexually transmitted diseases. A 2004 study suggested that Depo-Provera use increases the risk of Chlamydia and gonorrhea.[14] A more recent study conducted among 3800 African couples suggests that Depo-Provera doubles the risk of transmitting H.I.V. Other studies suggest that progesterone thins the lining of the vagina which increases the risk of H.I.V. contraction, while others suggest that Depo-Provera is being used instead of condoms.[15] More research needs to be conducted in this area to conclusively establish the link between Depo-Provera and H.I.V. For many women these risks outweigh the occurrence of an unwanted pregnancy. However, what needs to be clear is the unspoken intent behind these contraceptives. The primary intent is to reduce the "underclass".

7
BLACK LEADERSHIP AND BIRTH CONTROL: FROM GARVEY TO OBAMA

In the earliest phases of the birth control movement the prominent thought among white Americans was that blacks were not intelligent enough to utilize birth control methods. But from the moment that birth control was considered as an option to address black poverty it stood as a polarizing issue within the black community and among black leadership. Many African Americans were divided on the issue of birth control along economic class lines. The black intelligentsia and bourgeois advocated for birth control while working class blacks were more likely to oppose family planning based on religious grounds. Marcus Garvey, the blacknationalist and leader of the UNIA (Universal Negro Improvement Association), felt that contraceptives impeded the growth of the Negro race. Garvey felt that the strength of the Negro was largely dependent upon high birth rates. To Garvey, birth control equated to race genocide.[1] And, in 1934, at the Seventh Annual Convention of the UNIA a resolution was passed that condemned the use of birth control among blacks. Around the same period the scholar W.E.B. Du Bois maintained that birth control should be utilized as a means to raise the standard of living amongst blacks. Du Bois was no way void of an elitist perspective. He was particularly concerned with the birth rates of the poorest of blacks. Du Bois was not the only intellectual advocating the use of birth control among blacks.

Charles S. Johnson, the first black president of Fisk University, wrote in an article entitled, "A Question of Negro Health" that Negroes were in need of "eugenic discrimination".² Johnson also served on the National Advisory Council of the Birth Control Federation of America. E. Franklin Frazier believed that birth control would improve the black race as the poor and "mentally deficient" had fewer children.³ However, Frazier did not believe that birth control would have a eugenic effect, and was more deeply concerned with the decrease in the number of educated blacks. But not all black intellectuals agreed that birth control would be beneficial for the Negro population. Pathologist and University of Chicago professor Julian Lewis maintained that black survival was largely dependent on high birth rates and that birth control was race suicide.⁴

By the 1960's genocidal claims increased as birth control clinics sprung up throughout African American communities and compulsory sterilizations of black women on public assistance became commonplace. Many of these assertions of genocide were made by black militants and nationalist organizations. For example, the Nation of Islam printed numerous articles in its widely read publication *Muhammad Speaks* denouncing birth control as a genocidal weapon against blacks. In a 1965 article Elijah Muhammad went so far as to profess that Yakub, an evil scientist, was the first to use birth control to create the white race from the indigenous black nation.⁵ Despite this bizarre claim the N.O.I. was instrumental in raising awareness of reproductive abuse within the African American community. From a global perspective, El Hajj Malik El Shabbaz (Malcolm X) affirmed that family planning was being aimed at the peoples of the darker nations to reduce their numbers. His words seem prophetic in light of the NSSM-200 which described a strategy that is currently being implemented by the U.S. to limit the numbers of certain nations in order to have access to precious resources in the developing world. The Black Panther Party also purported the black genocide argument. In the *Black Panther*, readers were told that childbirth was a revolutionary act. Women were encouraged to bear healthy black warriors and men were told to dissuade their women from using birth control.⁶ However there were many women within the party who believed that despite government efforts to curtail black reproduction, reproductive rights should be solely in the hands of women. As women gained more power within the ranks of the Black Panther Party the position of the party changed regarding the use of birth control, but opposition to compulsory sterilization continued. The Black Power Conference of 1967 in Newark, New Jersey, largely orchestrated by Amiri Baraka, passed an anti-birth control resolution that equated birth control to black genocide. In Pittsburgh during the late sixties, the United Movement for Progress leader William "Bouie" Haden threatened to use dynamite to prevent the opening of birth control clinics in some of Pittsburgh's impoverished neighborhood. In an unlikely union Haden, a proponent of the genocide theory, Dr. Charles Greenlee, and Charles Owen Rice, a Caucasian Catholic priest of Holy Rosemary, led a successful anti-birth control campaign (1966-1969) in Pittsburgh. Through their efforts Pittsburgh declined federal funds for birth control clinics.

Dr. Martin Luther King Jr., the most renowned American civil rights leader, was an advocate of birth control but staunchly opposed abortion, referring to the practice of abortion in several speeches as a form of genocide. In 1966, King did accept the Margaret Sanger Award, however it is necessary to note that at this time Planned Parenthood maintained *at least publically* that abortion was dangerous to the mother, murder of life after it had began, and *not* birth control. Jesse Jackson, King's most eminent disciple, spoke some of the most indicting words ever uttered by a prominent civil rights leader against abortion. He consistently referred to abortion of black babies as murder and genocide. In an open letter written to Congress, Jackson opposed the utilization of government funds for the purpose of killing infants.[7] Jackson also wrote a 1000 word essay that was published in *Right to Life News*. In this article, Jackson argued that the question of the 20th Century is the question of life, and the inability to feel the pang of conscience concerning the issue of abortion is indicative of the moral decay of not only the individual but all of society.[8] However, during the early 80's this seemingly unyielding adversary to abortion joined the company of some of its most powerful proponents. Why did Jackson who considered his opposition to abortion as a matter of conscience alter his stance? Some maintain that Jackson's presidential bid would have been in jeopardy had he not tweaked his conscience to match that of the Democratic Party-line on abortion. This may explain how those such as Jackson and Al Sharpton who with their tongues claim to be preachers of the Gospel and with that same tongue politically defend a women's *right* to kill her unborn child. Both Jackson and Sharpton were unsuccessful in their attempts to ascend to the throne of the White House. But, what could not be accomplished in the their presidential bids was finally realized in the 2008 Presidential election of Barack Obama. Finally, the 44th president of the United States would be unlike all those that preceded him- he would be a man of color.

Initially, the election of Barack Obama meant many things to many different people. For some he meant the promise of a progressive stance from the presidential office. For others he represented the fulfillment of King's dream of equality for all Americans. And, for the most down trodden Blacks he was Moses. So far, his policies have been anything but progressive, in a "post-racial" America the median household wealth for whites is twenty times that of blacks[9], and for the most dispossessed blacks, Obama has been more like Pharaoh than Moses. But for the unborn child, Barack Obama, throughout his political career, has represented insecurity. As an Illinois Senator President Obama voted "present", which is the equivalent of voting "nay", on the following pieces of legislation:

1997

(1) SB230 Partial Birth Abortion Ban Act. Prohibits partial-birth abortions unless necessary to save the life of a mother whose life is endangered by a physical disorder, physical illness, or physical injury, provided that no other medical procedure would suffice for that purpose. Makes performance of a partial-birth abortion a Class 4 felony. Provides for a civil action by the father and maternal grandparents of the fetus. Prohibits prosecution of a woman on whom a partial-birth abortion is performed.

The egregiousness of a "present" vote on such legislation becomes evident with explanation of what a partial abortion actually is. The Intact Dilation and Extraction (IDX) procedure, vernacularly referred to as "partial-birth abortion" is an abortion done late in a woman's pregnancy. Over the course of two to three days the cervix is dilated through the use of laminaria tents or pitocin is used to induce labor. Once the cervix is adequately dilated forceps and an ultrasound are used to grab the leg of the unborn child. Sometimes the fetus is turned to the breech position. One or both legs of the fetus are pulled from the cervix, which is why this procedure is referred to as a "partial birth abortion". The abortionist extracts the rest of the body leaving only the head within the uterus. The abortionist makes an incision at the base of the skull, the opening is widened and then a suction catheter is used to suction out the fetus' brain. Once the brain is removed the skull collapses and can be passed through the cervix.

(2) HB0382 Partial Birth Abortion Ban Act. Prohibits partial-birth abortions unless necessary to save the life of a mother whose life is endangered by a physical disorder, physical illness, or physical injury, provided that no other medical procedure would suffice for that purpose. Makes performance of a partial-birth abortion a Class 4 felony. Provides for a civil action by the father and maternal grandparents of the fetus. Prohibits prosecution of a woman on whom a partial-birth abortion is performed. (Governor's Amendatory Veto message- Recommends deleting a provision allowing the father of a fetus or infant to maintain a civil action for damages based on a violation of the Partial-birth Abortion Ban Act.

2001

(3) HB1900 Parental Notice of Abortion Act. Provides that a person may not knowingly perform an abortion on a minor or on an incompetent person unless 48 hours notice has been given to an adult family member of the minor or incompetent person. Provides for expectations to the notice requirement, and provides a procedure for obtaining a judicial waiver of the notice requirement. Requires a minor's consent to an abortion, except in the case of a medical emergency. Provides for disciplinary action against a physician who willfully fails to provide the required notice before performing an abortion on a minor or on an incompetent person. Provides that unauthorized signing of a waiver of notice or the unlawful disclosure of confidential information is a Class C misdemeanor.

(4) SB 562 Parental Notice of Abortion Act. Provides that a person may not knowingly perform an abortion on a minor or on an incompetent person unless 48 hours notice has been given to an adult family member of the minor or incompetent person. Provides for expectations to the notice of the notice requirement. Requires a minor's consent to an abortion, except in the case of a medical emergency. Requires for disciplinary action against a physician who willfully fails to provide the required notice before performing an abortion on a minor or on an incompetent person. Provides that the unauthorized signing of a waiver of notice or the unlawful disclosure of confidential information is a Class C misdemeanor.

(5) SB 1093 Law to Protect Liveborn Children. Amends the Illinois Abortion Law of 1975. Provides that no abortion procedure that, in the medical judgment of the attending physician, has a reasonable likelihood of resulting in a live born child shall be undertaken unless there is in attendance a physician other than the physician performing or inducing the abortion who shall address the child's viability and provide medical care for the child. Provides that a physician inducing an abortion that results in a live born child shall provide for the soonest practicable attendance of a physician other than the physician performing or inducing medical care for the child. Provides that a live child born as a result of an abortion shall be fully recognized as a human person and that all reasonable measures consistent with good medical practice shall be taken to preserve the life and health of the child.

(6) SB 1094 Induced Birth Infant Liability Act. Provides that it is the intent of the General Assembly to protect the life of a child born alive as the result of an induced labor abortion. Provides that a parent of the child or the public guardian of the county in which a child was born alive after an induced labor abortion or any other abortion has a cause of action against any hospital, health care facility or health care provider that fails to provide medical care for the child after birth. Amends the State Finance Act. Creates the Neonatal Care and Perinatal Hospice Fund. Provides that, if a child does not survive, any remaining proceeds of an action shall be deposited into the Fund. Provides that the moneys in the fund shall be used, subject to appropriation, for neonatal care or perinatal hospice.

(7) SB 1095 Defines Born Alive infant. Defines "born-alive infant" to include every infant member of the species homo sapiens who is born alive at any stage of development. Defines "born alive" to mean the complete expulsion or extraction from the mother of an infant, at any stage of development, who after that expulsion or extraction breathes or has a beating heart, pulsation of the umbilical cord, or definite movement of voluntary muscles, regardless of whether the umbilical cord has been cut and regardless of whether the expulsion or extraction occurs as a result of natural or induced labor, cesarean section, or induced abortion.

Just as alarming as the President's votes of "present" as a senator in Illinois is President Obama's pick for his top science advisor. In 2008 the President appointed John Holdren Director of the White House Office of Science and Technology Policy and Assistant to the President for Science and Technology. Informally known as the president's "science czar" Holdren co-authored a book entitled, *Ecoscience: Population, Resources, Environment*. Within this text, Obama's top science advisor Holdren and his colleagues advocated the following[10]: 1) compulsory population control laws, including compulsory abortions under the U.S. Constitution 2) Children born out of wedlock should be put up for adoption, and possibly require expecting single mothers to have an abortion instead of adoption 3) sterilization of the population through the addition of sterilants to the water or food supply 4) Involuntary birth control, perhaps the development of a capsule that could be implanted under a women's skin to promote long-term sterilization The capsule could be implanted during the time of puberty and removed with governmental permission. 5) compulsory sterilization and/or forced abortions for individuals who cause "social deterioration" by way of overproduction 6) family size be dictated by the law 7) the development of an international superagency that could control the distribution of the planet's natural resources so that the birth limitations could be imposed upon all nations.

On Father's Day in 2008 Barack Obama stood before a vast crowd at the Apostolic Church of God in Chicago and blasted absentee fathers. A few weeks later, before an energized crowd at the 99th Annual NAACP Convention, and while under fire for his comments on Father's Day, Obama once again lectured the Black community on the importance of responsibility. This time he spoke of being an example of morality just as the African American community was an example for the nation during the Civil Rights movement. His stance concerning responsibility is problematic for two reasons. First, in retrospect, perhaps the focus on responsibility, which undoubtedly is a pressing issue within the black community, was addressed so adamantly because the Obama Administration would have no intention of confronting the challenges of poverty, unemployment, and risk of foreclosure that plagues the African American community. In other words Obama seems to be saying to the black community, "You are on your own!, (at least during this first term in office)." Obama has joined the ranks of the majority of American presidents who have failed to appropriately address the woes and tribulations of the nation's most dispossessed blacks. Second, it is the epitome of hypocrisy to deliver a harangue on moral responsibility with a 100% approval rating from NARAL.[11] How can you reprimand black fathers, on Father's Day about not taking care of their children, and simultaneously advocate the murder of children not yet born? This again is hypocrisy. Abortion is devastating the African American community. This decimation did not commence with Obama, but is certainly being furthered during the Obama Administration.

This critique of Obama on the issue of abortion is in no way an endorsement of white or black Republican Party candidates. It is necessary to make this point known because currently, the Right is conducting all out assaults on abortion providers such as Planned Parenthood and using the high black abortion rate as ammunition. However, it is naïve to think that the Grand Old Party is genuinely interested in the welfare of Blacks in this country. It is beneficial for the Republican Party to defund Planned Parenthood, not because it is an insidious organization that locates its clinics in predominantly minority neighborhoods to prey on black and brown people, nor is this a matter of fiscal responsibility. The Democratic Party funds Planned Parenthood, and in turn Planned Parenthood funds the Democratic Party with campaign contributions. A vast amount of these funds are allotted to individual candidates. Ultimately, Planned Parenthood funds the defeat of Republican candidates. This relationship between Democrats and organizations such as Planned Parenthood is the raison d'être for the GOP's opposition of government funding of abortion. This is why in largely black and brown cities anti-abortion signs are draped over building depicting young minority children with provocative phrases. It is important to understand that the historical relationships between the African American community and the dominant political parties have not been reciprocal. Both the Democratic and Republican parties have manipulated the black vote to yield political power when necessary or convenient. El Hajj Malik El Shabbazz (Malcolm X) was correct in his assessment that Negroes in America are "political chumps". Not much has changed even as a man of color resides in the White House and serves as the face of American empire.

Marcus Garvey (1887-1940)
Black Nationalist
Pan-Africanist
Founder of Universal Negro Improvement Association and African Communities Leauge (UNIA-ACL)

Jesse Jackson (1941-)
Civil Rights Activist
Baptist Minister
Founder of Rainbow/PUSH
Democratic Presidential Candidate in 1984 and 1988
Shadow Senator for the District of Columbia (1991-1997)

Barack Obama (1961-)
President of the United States (2009-)
Illinois State Senator (2005-2008)
Member of the Illinois Senate 13th District (1997-2004)

John Holdren (1944-)
Director of the Office of Science and Technology Policy
Co-author of *Ecoscience: Population, Resoureces, and Environment 1978*

8
WHY ROE V. WADE IS UNCONSTITUTIONAL

In a 7-2 decision the United States Supreme Court handed down rulings that legalized abortion in America. Prior to the January 22, 1973 *Roe v. Wade* ruling and the lesser known *Doe v. Bolton*[1] ruling that was issued on the same day, abortion was illegal in almost every state. The regulations on abortion in states where the practice was legal prior to these landmark cases were removed after the Court's ruling. Since 1973 there have been approximately 50 million abortions performed within the United States.[2] This chapter presents the reasons why Roe v. Wade is unconstitutional and should be overturned.

Exceeded Constitutional Authority

The Court exceeded its constitutional authority by making a law sanctioning abortion. According to the U.S. Constitution, the power to establish law is vested in Congress and is retained by the state legislatures. Although the power of judicial review is not explicitly granted to the Court by the Constitution, the authority to invalidate laws deemed unconstitutional has a long precedence that began with *Marbury v. Madison* (1803). With its Roe v. Wade ruling the High Court overstepped its role of determining if laws violate the constitutional rights of individuals. In this case the Court struck down laws it deemed not unconstitutional but rather bad social policy. In 1982, Justice Burger expressed the standard of the Court when he wrote:

> "Irrespective of what we may believe is wise or prudent policy in this difficult area, "the Constitution does not constitute us as 'Platonic Guardians' nor does it vest in this Court the authority to strike down laws because they do not meet our standards of desirable social policy, 'wisdom,' or 'common sense."[3]

The Right to Privacy

The Supreme Court based its ruling on the "right to privacy" which the Court maintained was guaranteed by the Constitution. The Court determined that while this right was not specifically mentioned in the Constitution it was implied in either the Fourteenth Amendment or the Ninth Amendment. However, the Court's finding that laws prohibiting abortion violated a women's right to privacy is not mentioned in the text of the Constitution, nor is it implied. In his dissenting opinion, Justice Byron White correctly attests:

> I find nothing in the language or history of the Constitution to support the Court's judgment. The Court simply fashions and announces a new constitutional right to pregnant mothers…and, with scarcely any reason or authority for its action, invests that right with sufficient substance to override most existing state abortion statutes. The upshot is that the people and the legislatures of the 50 states are constitutionally disentitled to weigh the relative importance of the continued existence and development of the fetus, on the one hand, against a spectrum of possible impacts on the mother, on the other hand. As an exercise of raw judicial power, the court perhaps has authority to do what it does today; but, in my view, its judgment is an improvident and extravagant exercise of the power of judicial review that the Constitution extends to this Court..

Nevertheless, Justice Harry Blackmun argues in the majority opinion:

> "The right of privacy, whether it be founded in the Fourteenth Amendment's concept of personal liberty and restrictions upon state action, as we feel it is, as the District Court determined, in the Ninth Amendment's reservation of rights to the people, is broad enough to encompass a woman's decision whether or not or not to terminate her pregnancy."

Even the concession of an implied right to privacy is problematic because of its broadness. A right to privacy that is expansive enough to encompass the act of abortion is thus applicable to practically every illegality outside of public view. If this is the case what other implied rights are there in the Constitution? Furthermore there is nothing private about an abortion. Justice Blackmum bonded the "right" to have an abortion with past court decisions that recognize privacy rights in the spheres of marriage, childrearing, procreation, and contraception use (*Loving v. Virginia*, *Skinner v. Oklahoma*, *Meyer v. Nebraska* and *Pierce* v. *Society of Sisters*, and *Griswold v. Connecticut* with abortion.) Marriage, childrearing, and procreation predate the laws of man and are inherent in the notions of liberty and the pursuit of happiness. Contraception use and abortion, although similar in terms of purpose, are not comparable in the realm of privacy. The later is done outside of the confines of a marital bedroom. The Court's use of the Ninth Amendment to justify the unspecified right to privacy that is inclusive of the right to have an abortion *contradicts* the right to life retained by the people in the Ninth Amendment.

The Question of When Life Begins

It is logical to assume that for the Court to determine the constitutionality of abortion, it first would have to settle the question of when life begins. However, the Court sidesteps this question entirely in order to sanction the act. Blackmun wrote:

> "We need not resolve the difficult question of when life begins. When those trained in the respective disciplines of medicine, philosophy, and theology are unable to arrive at any consensus, the judiciary, at this point in the development of man's knowledge, is not in a position to speculate as to the answer."[4]

Considering the possible destruction of life, how could the judiciary ethically overturn laws legalizing abortion if it was uncertain of when life commenced? Furthermore, Blackmun's assertion that no consensus existed concerning the issue of when life begins, at least in the areas of science and medicine, is simply untrue. In a Senate Judiciary committee meeting on the Human Life Bill the committee summarized the issue of when life begins as follows:

> "Physicians, biologists, and other scientists agree that conception marks the beginning of the life of a human being- a being that is alive and is a member of the human species. There is overwhelming agreement on this point in countless medical, biological, and scientific writings."[5]

The Supreme Court Assumed the Role of Legislature in Establishment of Trimester Framework

Blackmun claimed that it is was unnecessary to speculate on when life begins but does just that with his trimester framework.[6] By establishing a trimester framework, the Court assumed the role of a legislature. Again, the Court extended its constitutional authority according to Article VI, Section 2 of the U.S. Constitution. This arbitrary trimester framework stipulated the following: (1) the state may not regulate abortion for any reason during the first trimester when the privacy interest of the mother is the strongest. (2) During the second trimester, state regulation could only occur to protect the woman's health. (3) In the third trimester the state may regulate or prohibit abortion to protect the "potential" life of the child, except when abortion is necessary to preserve the health or life of the mother. In the majority opinion of Webster v. Reproductive Health Services Supreme Court Rehnquist denounced this arbitrary trimester framework. He stated:

> The key elements of the Roe framework trimesters and viability are not found in the text of the Constitution or in any place else one would expect to find a constitutional principle... the result has been a web of legal rules that have become increasingly intricate, resembling a code of regulations rather than a body of constitutional doctrine. As Justice White puts it, the trimester framework has left this Court to serve as the country's "ex

officio" medical board with powers to approve or disapprove medical and operative practices and standards throughout the United States.⁷

Unbeknownst to many Americans, in *Roe v. Wade's* companion case, *Doe v. Bolton*, the Supreme Court ruled that the state could not deny a woman's "right" to have an abortion after viability⁸ if abortion was deemed necessary to protect the health of the mother. The Court defined health as follows: "all factors-physical, emotional, psychological, familial, and the woman's age- relevant to the well-being of the patient."⁹ The use of this broad definition extended the right to have an abortion upon request during *any* month of pregnancy.

Misinterpretation of History

The Supreme Court's ruling that the unborn are nonpersons was largely influenced by its inaccurate historical interpretation of abortion. According to the historical observation of the Court, abortion was not a punishable crime from the earliest time of common law¹⁰ until the nineteenth century. And, abortion laws passed during the nineteenth century were ratified for the health of the mother, not the unborn child. Blackmun wrote:

> "It is undisputed that, at common law, abortion performed before "quickening"—the first recognizable movement of the fetus in utero, appearing usually from the 16th to the 18th week of pregnancy – was not an indictable offense."¹¹

Many legal scholars have pointed out that quickening, the moment in which the women feels the movements of the child in the womb, was an evidentiary test for the crime of abortion because this was the only method to ensure that a pregnancy did in fact exist because there were no pregnancy tests at the time. This did not mean, as the Court implies, that the unborn child was not considered a living human being. Blackmun based the erroneous historical analysis mainly on the thesis of Cyril C. Means, Jr. who was at one time the general counsel of the National Association for the Repeal of Abortion Laws (NARAL). To claim that abortion was not a crime in common law Means had the arduous task of refuting Edward

Coke[12] who regarded abortion as a " great misprision".[13] To support his position, Means uses the dismissals of abortion charges in two cases (*The Twinslayer's Case, & The Abortionist's Case*). However, it is more probable that these dismissals were a result of an inability to prove guilt, not the lawfulness of abortion. The Court in essence charges Coke with creating the crime of abortion. This is an example of how history is distorted. The Court concluded, "…it now appears doubtful that abortion was ever firmly established as a common-law crime even with respect to the destruction of a quick fetus."[14] The Court frames the differences in common law pre/post quickening abortions to mean that common law allowed women the latitude to abort their children during the early months of pregnancy. The truth of the matter is that the unborn were protected under common law. At the time, medically it was not necessarily accepted that life commenced at the moment of conception and certainly could not be proven before the time of quickening. However, the unborn were protected by the law even when the predominant thought was that life began at the moment of quickening. Blackstone wrote:

> "Life is the immediate gift of God, a right inherent by nature in every individual; and it begins in contemplation of law as soon as the infant is able to stir in the mother's womb. For if a woman is quick with child, and by a potion, or otherwise, killeth it in her womb…this, though not murder, was by the ancient law homicide or manslaughter. But at present it is not looked upon in quite so atrocious a light, though it remains a very heinous misdemeanor."[15]

The discovery of the ovum in 1827 proved that conception was the beginning of life. Not long after the term "quick with child" became synonymous with the moment of conception. In 1837, Parliament ratified an abortion statute that was void of an evidentiary requirement and made abortion at any time punishable by law. This scientific advancement led to the protection of the unborn at any stage of pregnancy. Notwithstanding, the Court provided a distorted perception of common law that implies that a lack of prosecution equates to legal right. To support the fallacy that, "few state courts called upon to interpret their laws in the late nineteenth and early twentieth century did focus on the state's interests in protecting the woman's health rather than in preserving the embryo and fetus"

Blackmun cited one 1858 New Jersey case. The Court ignores the fact that the circumstances surrounding an illegal act impacts the punishment for that crime. (e.g. lesser punishment for the crime of murder committed by an individual deemed legally insane). This lesser judgment does not indicate that a particular act is legal. But this is just what the Court implies in its interpretation of the New Jersey case. In addition, the Court also ignores the numerous court decisions of the same time that explicitly affirm, and others that imply, that abortion statutes were for the protection of the unborn child.[16]

The Unborn as Nonpersons and the Use of the 14th Amendment

Blackmun's statement, "the unborn have never been recognized in the law as persons in the whole sense" is reminiscent of a time in American history in which individuals were arbitrarily deemed as nonpersons or not fully human. In the *Dred Scott v. Sanford* (1857) case the Supreme Court ruled that persons of African descent brought into the United States as slaves, and their descendants were not protected by the U.S. Constitution and were not citizens, nor could they ever be. Thus the Court ruled that Scott was not a citizen within the meaning of the U.S. Constitution at the time of its adoption. The majority opinion written by Chief Justice Taney stated the following:

> They had for more than a century before been regarded as beings of an inferior order, altogether unfit to associate with the white race, either in social or political relations; and so far inferior, that they had no rights which the white man was bound to respect; and that the negro might justly and lawfully be reduced to slavery for his benefit.

The contrariness of the Court's decision, in the case of *Roe v. Wade*, is quite telling in its use of the Fourteenth Amendment. The broad definition of citizenship in the Citizenship Clause of the Fourteenth Amendment partially overruled the *Dred Scott v. Sanford* decision, which held that Blacks could not be citizens. It is ironic that the Amendment used to overrule the Dred Scott decision which held that blacks were nonpersons and consequently non citizens was utilized in Roe v. Wade to treat the unborn as "beings of inferior order who have not rights which the born are bound to respect." Consider the similarities in each decision (*Dred Scott v. Sanford* and *Roe v. Wade*) that rendered blacks and the unborn as nonpersons.

'Citizens' and 'Persons' does not apply to African Americans and the Unborn

Dred Scott v. Sanford (1857)
"… a negro, whose ancestors were imported into this country, and sold as slaves… were not intended to be included under the word **'citizens'** in the Constitution, and can, therefore, claim none of the rights and privileges which that instrument provides for and secures to citizens of the United States."

Roe v. Wade (1973)
"The word 'person,' as used in the Fourteenth Amendment, does not include the unborn… [T]he unborn have never been recognized in the law as **persons** in the whole sense."

Right to Privacy

Dred Scott v. Sanford (1857)
A slave is the property of the master and the Constitution has "provided for the protection of **private property** in the law as persons in the whole sense."

Roe v. Wade (1973)
"This **right of privacy**… is broad enough to encompass a woman's decision whether or not to terminate her pregnancy."

Historical justification for slavery and abortion

Dred Scott v. Sanford (1857)
"…the negro might justly and lawfully be reduced to slavery for his benefit."

Roe v. Wade (1973)
"There is also the distress for all concerned, associated with the unwanted child, and there is the problem of bringing a child into a family unable, psychologically, and otherwise to care for it."

The *Roe v. Wade* decision is perhaps the most egregious Supreme Court judgment in U.S. history. This is particularly true in regard to its impact on African Americans. But perhaps, this was not by accident. Perhaps it was the Court's intent to be "Platonic Guardians" indeed and pass a type of legislation that would lead to the "culling" of certain populations. In a 2009 New York Times Magazine interview Supreme Court Justice Ruth Bader Ginsberg stated that during the time of *Roe v. Wade* she assumed that the controversial case would be used to allow Medicaid funding for abortions in order to curtail the numbers of populations that were considered undesirable.[17] It would be naïve to believe that Supreme Court decisions are solely based on constitutionality or unconstitutionality. Take for instance the *Brown v. Board of Education* (1954) decision that declared separate public schools to be unconstitutional. The Court was made aware that school integration was an important factor in maintaining American world dominance. The Justice Department maintained that racial segregation had "an adverse effect upon our relations with other countries. Racial discrimination furnishes grist for the Communist propaganda mills, and it raises doubts even among friendly nations as to the intensity of our devotion to the democratic faith."[18] *Brown v. Board of Education* was bigger than black and white children being educated in the same classroom. It was a matter of, at least in part, combating the spread of Communism. Perhaps *Roe v. Wade,* as Justice Ginsburg stated, was at least in part a matter of population control.

Byron Raymond White (1917-2002)
Associate Justice of the United States Supreme Court
In Office (April 16, 1962 - June 28, 1993)
Roe v. Wade (1973) Senior Dissenting Justice

Justice Harry A. Blackmun, (1908-1999)
Associate Justice of the United States Supreme Court
In Office (June 9, 1970-August 3, 1994)
Roe v. Wade (1973) Wrote the Court's Opinion

Ruth Bader Ginsburg (1933-)
Associate Justice of the United States Supreme Court
In Office (August 10, 1993-)

Roger B. Taney (1777-1864)
Chief Justice of the United States Supreme Court
In Office (March 15, 1836- October 12, 1864)
Delivered the Supreme Court decision *Dred Scott v. Sanford* (1857)

Dred Scott (1795-1858)
Plaintiff in the *Dred Scott v. Sanford* (1857) U.S. Supreme Court Case

ELISHA J. ISRAEL

9
BIBLICAL ARGUMENT AGAINST ABORTION

And the angel said unto her, Fear not, Mary; for thou hast found favour with God. And, behold, thou shalt conceive in thy womb, and bring forth a son, and shalt call his name Jesus. He shall be great, and shall be called the Son of the Highest: and the Lord God shall give unto him the throne of his father David: And he shall reign over the house of Jacob for ever; and of his kingdom there shall be no end. (Luke 1:30-33)

The Word of God speaks very clearly on a variety of topics, but what about abortion? What does the Bible have to say concerning this divisive issue? One could argue that the Bible says nothing about induced abortion, because induced abortion is not specifically mentioned in the text. However, upon examination of the Holy Scriptures concerning subjects such as the sanctity of human life and the blessings of children, it becomes quite apparent that abortion is contrary to the will of God. The Bible speaks volumes concerning the immorality of abortion. Upon reading the following Biblical arguments it will become crystal clear that it is antithetical to profess belief in the God of Abraham, Isaac, and Jacob, and simultaneously support a women's "right" to choose.

1 God is Involved in the Development of the Child in the Womb

What all people should understand is that there is a Creator, and all that is done against the will of God will be accounted for. This Creation did not come into existence from a "big bang", but rather emerged out of the works of this Creator. Mankind is one of the works in which He is intricately involved. Men of God testified of this fact in the Scriptures. In the 139th Psalm, David acknowledges the sovereignty of God in his individual existence. The Psalmist wrote, "For thou hast possessed my reins: thou hast covered me in my mother's womb. I will praise thee; for I am fearfully and wonderfully made: marvelous are thy works; and that my soul knoweth right well. My substance was not hid from thee, when I was made in secret, and curiously wrought in the lowest parts of the earth. Thine eyes did seem my substance, yet being unperfect; and in thy book all my members were written, which in continuance were fashioned, when as yet there was none of them."[19] David unmistakably declares that it was God who formed him in his mother's womb. A parallel between his own creation in the womb and the creation of Adam is made when he penned, "I was made in secret, and curiously wrought in the lowest parts of the earth." This is an allusion to Genesis 2 which reads, "God created man from the dust of the ground and breathed into his nostrils the breath of life and man became a living soul."[20] Job also professes that it was God who formed him in his mother's womb. The scripture poetically reads, "What then shall I do when God riseth up? And when he visiteth, when shall I answer him? Did not he that made me in the womb make him? and did not one fashion us in the womb?[21]

The prophets had similar declarations. The Prophet Isaiah professed: "Thus saith the LORD, thy redeemer, and he that formed thee from the womb, I am the LORD that maketh all things; that stretcheth forth the heavens alone; that spreadeth abroad the earth by myself".[22] Jeremiah wrote the following concerning his sanctification as a prophet: "Before I formed thee in the belly I knew thee; and before thou camest forth out of the womb I sanctified thee, and I ordained thee a prophet unto the nations.[23] Paul, the Apostle to the Gentiles, was also sanctified before his birth. In his epistle to Galatia he informs the church there that "...it pleased God, who separated me from my mother's womb, and called me by his grace, To reveal his Son in me, that I might preach him among the heathen;..."[24]

Regarding John the Baptist, the angel Gabriel told Zachariah that, "For he shall be great in the sight of the Lord, and shall drink neither wine nor strong drink; and he shall be filled with the Holy Ghost, even from his mother's womb."[25] In these instances we see evidence of God's divine oversight in the lives of individuals prior to their birth. So, from a biblical perspective, human life definitely begins prior to delivery into the world.

2 Procreation commanded by God and children seen as a blessing

The first commandment given to man was to reproduce. In Genesis it is written, "And God blessed them, and God said unto them, Be fruitful, and multiply, and replenish the earth..."[26] God ordained and commanded the continuous procreation of man. The fruit that emerges from God's mandate is considered to be a blessing.[27] Below are scriptural references that attest to this fact.

Children are a Blessing

Genesis 17:15 And God said unto Abraham, As for Sarai thy wife, thou shalt not call her name Sarai, but Sarah shall her name be 16 And I will bless her, and give thee a son also of her: yea, I will bless her, and she shall be a mother of nations; kings of people shall be of her.

Genesis 25:21 And Isaac entreated the Lord for his wife, because she was barren; and the Lord was entreated of him, and Rebekah his wife conceived.

Genesis 33:4 And Esau ran to meet him (Jacob), and embraced him, and fell on his neck, and kissed him: and they wept. 5 And he lifted up his eyes, and saw the women and the

Genesis 20:17 So Abraham prayed unto God: and God healed Abimelech, and his wife, and his maidservants; and they bare children. 18 For the Lord had fast closed up all the wombs of the house of Abimelech, because of Sarah Abraham's wife.

Genesis 30:20 And Leah said, God hath endued me with a good dowry; now will my husband because I have born him six sons...

Genesis 48:8 And Israel beheld Joseph's sons, and said, Who are these? 9 And Joseph said unto his father, They are my sons, whom God hath given me in children; and said, Who are those with thee? And he said, The children which God hath graciously given thy servant.

Deuteronomy 7:12 Wherefore it shall come to pass, if ye hearken to these judgments, and keep, and do them, that the Lord thy God shall keep unto thee the covenant and the mercy which he sware unto thy fathers.

14 Thou shalt be blessed above all people: there shall not be male or female barren among you, or among your cattle.

this place. And he said, Bring them, I pray thee, unto me, and I will bless them.

Exodus 23:25 And ye shall serve the Lord your God, and he shall bless thy bread, and thy water; and I will take sickness away from the midst of thee. 26 There shall nothing cast their young, nor be barren, in thy land the number of thy days I will fulfill.

3 Judgment Concerning Child Killed in the Womb

If men strive, and hurt a woman with child, so that her fruit depart from her, and yet no mischief follow: he shall be surely punished, according as the woman's husband will lay upon him; and he shall pay as the judges determine. And if any mischief follow, then thou shalt give life for life.
(Exodus 21:22-23)

According to the law of God the unborn child has the same status as a baby that is born. If men engaged in a physical altercation and struck a pregnant woman causing her to give birth prematurely, it would constitute a fine. However, the law required a life for life, if the altercation caused the woman to lose the fruit of her womb. Thus, the unborn child has the same legal status as a born child. Some who hold a different interpretation of this scripture would argue that the verses refer to accidental miscarriage. This suggests that the unborn child does not share the same legal status as a child that is born, hence the fine. However, this interpretation is problematic for two reasons. First, the Hebrew word for miscarry is not used in this instance. It is most likely that this is referring to a premature birth. Secondly, even if this interpretation was correct, it does not justify abortion. Miscarriage under the circumstances described in this law would be *inadvertent*, whereas induced abortion is *intentional*. Also, as has already been stated, the legal status of the child in the womb is no different than that of the child that has been birthed into the world. This would indicate that the 6th Commandment, "Thou shalt not kill"[28], which is interpreted properly as thou shalt not murder, also applies in the case of abortion. So, from a biblical standpoint, to abort is to murder.

4 What about instances of rape and incest?

Abortion advocates frequently cite instances of rape and incest to buttress their position to justify abortion. However, very few women have abortions because of rape or incest. For example, in a 2004 study, which surveyed 1209 women on the reasons why they sought abortion, 1% of respondents gave rape as a reason and less than 0.5% cited incest. [29] The sad reality is that the vast majority of women have abortions because of the complicating factors associated with having a child (e.g. "can't afford a baby, "would interfere with school", or insufficient support from partner, etc.). Thus**, abortion is being used in many cases as a method of birth control.** The intention here is not to in any way trivialize rape, incest, or for that matter the complications that accompany inopportune pregnancies. However, dire straits, even the appalling occurrences of rape and incest fail to legitimate the act of abortion. The Holy Bible unequivocally reveals to us that the murder of a child as a consequence of the parent's iniquity is unrighteous judgment. Ezekiel writes concerning this standpoint, "Yet say ye, Why? Doth not the son bear the iniquity of the father? When the son hath done that which is lawful and right, and hath kept all my statutes, and hath done them, he shall surely live."[30] Ezekiel goes on to write, "The soul that sinneth, it shall die. The son shall not bear the iniquity of the father, neither shall the father bear the iniquity of the son: the righteousness of the righteous shall be upon him, and the wickedness of the wicked shall be upon him."[31] Moses wrote, "The fathers shall not be put to death for the children, neither shall the children be put to death for the fathers: every man shall be put to death for his own sin."[32] The woman who is raped or molested is an innocent victim. We would think it absurd to kill a woman based on her victimization. And yet, this is what happens in the case of abortion. The wrongdoing of the father is borne by the child and thus sin is compounded.

5 Abortion is contrary to the reason for man's existence

Let us consider man's potential within the cycle of life. It is not only to reproduce other men and women; it is ultimately to become what our Father is. The potential of mankind is to become God. In Psalms it is written, "I have said, ye are gods; and all of you are children of the most High."[33] When Jesus himself was accused of blasphemy He responded with the following: "...Is it not written in your law, I said, Ye are gods? If he called them gods, unto whom the word of God came, and the scripture cannot be broken; Say ye of him, whom the Father hath sanctified, and sent into the world, Thou blasphemest; because I said, I am the Son of God?[34] He is the first begotten of the dead. He became God once again through the resurrection, and so shall others at His Second Advent. For it is written again, "For our conversation is in heaven; from whence also we look for the Saviour, the Lord Jesus Christ: Who shall change our vile body, that it may be fashioned like unto his glorious body, according to the working whereby he is able even to subdue all things unto himself."[35] Daniel writes of the resurrection and declares that those who awake to everlasting life will "...shine as the brightness of the firmament; and they that turn many to righteousness as the stars of heaven."[36] If we are to have a body like Jesus, we will have a body that is celestial and immortal- a body like God's. Man was created in the image and likeness of God. God was not simply creating playthings; in the creation of mankind God was and is procreating. So, to abort the unborn child is to destroy that which has the potential to become God. Was it not Satan's desire to destroy the creation of God?

Conclusion

The Holy Scriptures make two things abundantly clear. First, the constant proclamation that America is a godly nation as she sanctions the act of abortion is duplicitous. The prevalence of abortions is indicative of the moral depravity and godlessness that is so pervasive in American society today. America is no different from ancient civilizations of which Leckey writes, "The practice of abortion was one to which few persons in antiquity attached any deep feeling of condemnation."[37] The persons to whom he refers to were pagan worshippers who knew not the true and living God. Today in like fashion, without a pang of conscience, America destroys the most vulnerable of her society. Second, what is truly alarming is the deafening silence of clergy on the issue of abortion. As the plague of abortion has killed millions, too few words of dissent have been uttered by those who claim to be God's stewards. I ask, what is the function of the watchman? Is it not to sound the alarm of the dangerous nature of sin? Indeed, abortion is sin and the watchmen's failure to blow the trumpet concerning this egregious act places physical as well as spiritual lives in grave peril.

10
SACRIFICING OUR FUTURE (AN APPEAL TO CONSCIENCE)

Who is to blame for the black infant holocaust? Should the fault be laid entirely at the feet of Malthusian eugenicists and racists who believe it necessary to exterminate the darker races in order to preserve the superior Nordic stock, or legislators and politicians who are only interested in cutting welfare roles, or companies looking to profit from implanting young black girls with harmful types of birth control? All of the aforementioned undoubtedly share some culpability. However, it is improbable that the millions of black abortions since 1973 could have occurred without *our complicity*. This is a searing indictment but an appropriate one. Pro-choice advocates are quick to argue that unintended pregnancy is the reason for the elevated rates of abortions in the black community. It is true that African American women have the highest rates of unintended pregnancy. However, that argument fails to dig to the root cause of mass abortions. High abortion rates which correlate with high rates of unintended pregnancies suggest that a state of moral depravity exists within the black community. Let me be clear, I in no way discount the function of white supremacy to further exacerbate poverty which also has a direct correlation with unintended pregnancy and abortion. Furthermore, no rational American black descendant of slaves should be taken aback by the insidious efforts to control our reproduction. This type of oppression is congruent with the desire to control our reproduction in a manner that was socially and economically beneficial to the white power structure. Nevertheless, what each and every one of us should find appalling is our inappropriate response to white supremacy. Our response has been to abort our children at astronomical rates. This propensity to destroy our progeny indicates the acceptance of moral relativism (belief that socio-historical context determines what behavior is moral or immoral) concerning sexual behavior and abortion, and outright nihilism (the rejection of any moral truth) among many of us. Our willingness to deny or ignore the immorality of abortion is part of this larger problem of moral relativism and nihilism within the Black community. And, these decaying moral principles are being manifested in a number of devastating ways in addition to abortion.

STD rates among African American Adults

A 2009 report by the CDC on sexual transmitted diseases revealed some disturbing information concerning STD's and African Americans. In 2009, approximately 71% of all reported cases of gonorrhea occurred among African Americans. This is a rate 20.5 times higher than the rate among Caucasians. In this same year 52.4% of all cases of syphilis were among blacks. This is a rate 22.4 percentage points higher than whites.[1] African Americans also have higher rates of Chlamydia. In 2009, 48% of all reported Chlamydia cases were among blacks.[2]

STD rates among African American Teens

The CDC reported in 2009 that African American teenage boys are having sex at greater rates (72%) than Hispanics (53%) and whites (40%).[3] Black teenage girls are 2-3 times more likely to give birth than white teens. A 2008 CDC report revealed that more than 3 million teenage females in America have at least one sexually transmitted disease. This study focused on the most common STD's in teenage girls, which are Human papillomavirus (HPV), Chlamydia, herpes simplex virus, and trichomoniasis.[4] Researchers found that 48% of African American teenage girls had at least one STD compared to 20% of white teenage girls. In other words, according to this study, one in two African American teenage girls has an STD.

HIV/AIDS Epidemic

African Americans have been more devastated by HIV than any other ethnic group. By the end of 2007, blacks accounted for almost half (46%) of all diagnoses of HIV. In 2006, African Americans accounted for 45% of all new HIV infections.
1 in 16 black men and 1 in 30 black women can expect to be diagnosed with HIV in his or her lifetime. Men that have sex with men accounted for 63% of all new HIV infections among black men. In this same year HIV was the ninth leading cause of death among black men and the third leading killer among black men and women aged 35-44.[5]

Children Born Out of Wedlock

In a 1965 controversial study entitled "The Negro Family: The Case For National Action" the assistant Labor secretary of Labor Daniel Moynihan reported that 25% of black children were being born out-of-wedlock. More recent figures suggest that around 70% of African American children are born out of wedlock.[6]

Multiple Father Type of Family

A recent study of nearly 4000 women over a twenty seven year period revealed that 59% of African American mothers had children by more than one father.[7] The multiple-father type of family structure in the African American community is the accepted norm rather than the exception. Seventy-two percent of African American infants are born out-of-wedlock. This number has soared since 1965.

Black Infant Holocaust

One in five births worldwide end in abortion and approximately 37 million abortions are performed annually worldwide. Most of these abortions occur in the developed part of the world. From 1973 to 2008 there were approximately 50 million abortions in the United States. According to the Center for Disease Control (CDC) between 1973 and 2007 there have been approximately 13 million African Americans. To put this in perspective that is 33% of the current African American population. Had it not been for the high prevalence of abortion, the African American population would be closer to 50 million. African American women received 35% of all abortions in 2010 and are five times more likely to have an abortion than white women.[8] In some states the numbers are even more staggering. For instance, in 2006 57.4% of abortions in Georgia were performed on Black women whom comprised only 30% of the population.[9] A recent study by the New York Health Department showed that in 2009 New York women birthed 126,744 babies, suffered 11,620 miscarriages, and had **87,273** abortions.[10] Two out of every five pregnancies (41%) ended in abortion, two times the national average. **Fifty nine percent of African American pregnancies in the city ended in abortion.** As astounding as the 2009 data is, abortion rates were actually higher in the year 2000. The following table shows the number of black abortions from 1973-2007.[11]

Table I Number of Abortions 1973-2007 According the CDC

Year	Legal Abortions	Percentage of Black Abortions	Number of Black Abortions
1973	615,831	27.5%	169,354
1974	763,476	30.9%	235,914.1
1975	954,853	32.2%	307,462.67
1976	988,267	33.4%	330,081.178
1977	1,079,430	33.6%	362,688.48
1978	1,157,776	33%	382,066.08
1979	1,251,921	31.1%	389,347.43
1980	1,297,066	30.1%	390,579.41
1981	1,303,760	30.1%	392,431.76
1982	1,303,980	31.5%	410,753.7

1983	1,286,987	32.4%	416,983.79
1984	1,333,521	32.6%	434,727.85
1985	1,328,570	29.8%	395,913.9
1986	1,328,112	28.7%	381,168.14
1987	1,353,671	29.3%	396,625.6
1988	1,371,285	31.1%	426,469.64
1989	1,396,658	31.2%	435,757.30
1990	1,429,247	31.9%	455,929.79
1991	1,388,937	32.5%	451,404.53
1992	1,359,146	33.9	460,750.49
1993	1,330,414	34.9%	464,314.49
1994	1,267,415	34.7%	439,793.01
1995	1,210,983	35%	423,844.05
1996	1,225,937	35.3%	435,207.6
1997	1,186,039	35.9%	425,788
1998	884,273	37.3%	329,834
1999	861,790	37.3%	321,447.67
2000	857,475	36.3%	311,263.43
2001	853,485	36.6%	312,375.51
2002	854,122	36.6%	312,608.65

2003	848,163	37.1%	314,668,47
2004	839,226	38.2%	320,584.33
2005	820,151	36.9%	302,635.72
2006	846,181	36.4%	308,009.88
2007	827,609	36.5%	302,077.285

Approximate Number of Black Abortions between 1973 and 2007
12,636,193

In 2008, according to the Guttmacher Institute, there were 1.21 million abortions in the United States and 30% of these were performed on African American women.[12] In this year African American women averaged 994 abortions per day. To put this in perspective, in the years between 1882 and 1968, known as the "Lynching Century", the Tuskegee Institute recorded 3,466 lynchings of African Americans. Today, through abortion that number 3,446 is surpassed in about four days. Abortion is in reality the leading killer of black Americans. In any given year since 1973, the number of abortions surpassed the amount of deaths of the 10 leading causes of death for African Americans. Since 1973, more blacks have died from abortion than from deaths resulting from heart disease, violent crime, HIV/AIDs, cancer, accidents, and diabetes combined.

Table II Ten Leading Causes of Death among African Americans 2006[13]

Abortion	308,009
Diseases of the Heart	72,253
Malignant Neoplasms	63,082
Cerebrovascular Disease	17,045
Unintentional Injuries	13,917
Diabetes Mellitus	12,813
Homicide	9,032
Nephritis Neophrotic Syndrome, and Neophrosis	8,397
Chronic Lower Respiratory Diseases	7,730
Human Immunodeficiency Virus (HIV) Disease	6,854
Septicemia	6,108
Total	**597,980**

Complicit in Our Own Destruction

So what should we do as a people to thwart the savage slaying of millions of black innocents? First, let us begin with that which is futile. We can no longer appeal to the conscience of an immoral power structure. The answer to this dilemma lay not in yelling at the top of our lungs that this is egregious, this program to control our reproduction unjust, the practices of corporations and the state apparatus, sinister. After centuries of oppression we should expect nothing less from our adversaries. The fact of the matter remains that the current efforts to kill black children requires *our complicity*. We cannot continue to deny our role in this holocaust. We must do the difficult work of self-examination. We must look within our very souls and confront a moral decadence that allows the unconscionable killing of our most defenseless. We must begin to declare that there is no justifiable homicide when it comes to our children. We must begin to reevaluate our standards concerning sex, marriage, and familial relationships. The moral compass currently being used is leading us down a path paved with high rates of sexually transmitted diseases, dysfunctional familial structures, and mass abortions.

The Failure of the Black Church

In the past forty years there have been millions of black abortions, and yet the black Christian church has been relatively silent. It stands to reason that the church, more than any other institution in society, is positioned to address moral decadence. Moral decadence, particularly in the area of black male-female relationships and family structures, is the root cause of mass abortions, high rates of STDs, and vast numbers of children born out of wedlock. Unfortunately, the Christian black church has failed to appropriately address the moral crisis within black male-female relationships and family structures. These relationships and structures should be guided by a value system based on the spiritual tenets of the Holy Scriptures. Is it not the duty of the minister to uncompromisingly preach the word of God in order to prick the moral conscience? But today, as in the days of Isaiah, "His watchmen are blind: they are all ignorant, they are all dumb dogs, they cannot bark; sleeping, lying down, loving to slumber. Yea, they are greedy dogs which can never have enough, and they are shepherds that cannot understand: they all look to their own way, every one for his gain, from his quarter." Today, sin reigns because to preach an uncompromising gospel and to hold fast to God's law is simply not lucrative. So the itching ears of the sheep are soothed through deceit, and sinful acts like fornication and abortion are not admonished. But, the pastors who line their pockets by tolerating iniquity are not solely to blame. Every self professing Christian should realize that church attendance must be more than an emotional escape from the harsh reality of life. Nor should one attend church because he or she has been lured in by disingenuous assurances of monetary prosperity. Church is not a fashion show, a networking opportunity, the after-party following a night of drunken wantonness, or a baby-sitting service. It is the place where men and women should be instructed in the ways of life according to the word of God. Regrettably, the Holy Bible is treated as if it is a book of Jewish fables and not a manual for living. Yet, within its cover we find the knowledge of self, and liberation as a people, for it is our story. Through the Word of God we find guidance on how to walk in this life so that we do those things pleasing in His sight.

The significance of the institution of marriage as it is outlined in the Scriptures cannot be overstated. Just as the cell is the building block of life, the institution of marriage is the bedrock of human society. From the time of man's inception the family structure began with the covenanted union between a man and a woman. The state of this union significantly shapes the familial unit, community, and inevitably all of society. When there is a crisis between the man and woman; family, community, and society are also in crisis. This is indeed the case in the black community. The current condition of black male and female relationships and the family unit is a measure of inadequacy of spiritual leaders and institutions that fail to shape values and social mores that are based on the divine revelation of Scripture. The increasing failure of the black church to shape our moral outlook regarding sex, marriage, and child rearing is evident in the staggering statistics already mentioned (i.e. HIV/AIDS, abortion rates, out-of-wedlock births).

What are the benefits of being married? Black married individuals are less likely to experience emotional problems in comparison to unmarried blacks. They also experience more happiness, and fulfillment. Statistics also indicate that marriage increases economic status of black families. Children living with their married parents are less likely to live in poverty, have higher self esteem, are more likely to delay sexual intercourse and pregnancy, have increased educational opportunities, and are less likely to abort their children. We must affirm the dependence of black women on black men and black men on black women. We came in the hulls of ships together, worked the fields together, endured the lash together, stood on segregated buses together, and comforted one another during all that we have been confronted with-together. We need each other now, more than ever. Together, we must look to rebuild ourselves and our communities for the sake of our descendants. Rebuilding the relationship between black men and women and using the Holy Scriptures as our moral guide is essential in thwarting the mass killing of black innocents.

NOTES

Chapter 1 Control of Black Reproduction During Slavery

[1] Deuteronomy 28:68.

[2] Elisha J. Israel, *Into Egypt Again With Ships: A Message to the Forgotten Israelites (African Americans)* (United States: CreateSpace, 2009), 43-47.

[3] Department of Commerce and Labor Bureau of the Census, *A Century of Population Growth: From the First Census of the United states to the Twelfth 1790-1900* (Wash., D.C.: Government Printing Office, 1909), 132.

[4] United States Bureau of Census, *Preliminary Report on the Eighth Census, 1860, of the United States* (Wash., D.C.: Government Printing Office, 1862), 133.

[5] Ira Berlin, *Many Thousands Gone: The First Two Centuries of Slavery in North America* (United States: Harvard University Press, 1998), 126- 127.

[6] William Goodell, *The American Slave Code in Theory and Practice: Its Distinctive Features Shown by Its Statutes, Judicial Decisions, and Illustrative Facts* (New York: American and Foreign Anti-Slavery Society, 1853), part 1, ch. 5, 84: Theodore D. Weld et al, ed., *Slavery as It Is: Testimony of a Thousand Witnesses* (New York: American Anti-Slavery Society, 1839), 175.

[7] Frederick Douglass, *Narrative of the Life of Frederick Douglass* (New York: Dover Publications, Inc., 1995), 37.

[8] Frederick Law Olmstead, *Journey and Explorations in the Cotton Kingdom, vol. 1* (London: S. Low, Son & Co., 1861), 57-58.

[9] Leonard Bacon, *Slavery Discussed in Occasional Essays From 1833-1846* (New York: Baker and Scribner, 1846), 94.

[10] John Elliot Cairnes, *The Slave Power: Its Character, Career and Probable Designs Being an Attempt to Explain the Real Issues Involved in the American Contest* (London: Macmiilan and Co., 1863), 1834.

[11] A.H. Conrad & J.R. Meyer, *The Economics of Slavery in the Antebellum South and Other Studies in Econometric History* (Piscataway, NJ: Aldine Publishing Company, 1964).

[12] *Slave Narratives: A Folk History of Slavery in the United States from Interviews with Former Slaves, Arkansas,* Part 6 (Washington, DC: Kessinger Publishing, 2004), 154.

[13] *Born in Slavery: Slave Narratives from the Federal Writers' Project, 1936-1938, Texas Narratives,* vol. 16, part 1, 218.

[14] *Born in Slavery: Slave Narratives from the Federal Writers' Project, 1936-1938, Texas Narratives,* vol. 16, part 1, 299.

[15] *Born in Slavery: Slave Narratives from the Federal Writers' Project, 1936-1938, Texas Narratives,* vol. 16, part 4, 189.

[16] *Born in Slavery: Slave Narratives from the Federal Writers' Project, 1936-1938, North Carolina Narratives,* vol. 11, part 1, 31.

[17] *Born in Slavery: Slave Narratives from the Federal Writers' Project, 1936-1938, Texas Narratives,* vol. 11, part 1, 137.

[18] *Born in Slavery: Slave Narratives from the Federal Writers' Project, 1936-1938, Florida Narratives,* vol. 3, 128.

[19] Dorothy Roberts, *Killing the Black Body,* (New York: Pantheon Books, a division of Random House, Inc., 1997), 25.

[20] *American Slavery, As It Is: Testimony of a Thousand Witnesses* (New York: American Anti-Slavery Society, 1839), 15.

[21] *American Cotton Planter and the Soil of the South,* vol. 1 (Montgomery, AL: Underwood & Cloud, 1857), 295.

[22] Samuel Sands, *The American Farmer, and Spirit of the Agricultural Journals of the Day, Devoted to the Interests of the Farmers, Planters & Horticulturists of the United States* (Baltimore: Samuel Sands, Publisher), 78.

[23] Moses Grandy, *Narrative of the Life of Moses Grandy, Late a Slave in the United States of America* (Boston: O. Johnson Publishing Co., 1844), 18.

[24] *Born in Slavery: Slave Narratives from the Federal Writers' Project, 1936-1938, Arkansas Narratives,* vol. 2, 375.

[25] Junius P. Rodriguez, *Slavery in the United States: A Social, Political, and Historical Encyclopedia,* vol. 1. (ABC-CLIO: Santa Barbara, CA, 2007), 347.

[26] Herbert George Gutman, *The Black Family in Slavery and Freedom, 1750-1925.* (New York: Pantheon Books, 1976), 81.

[27] Deborah Gray White, *Ar'n't I a Woman?: Female Slaves in the Plantation South* (New York: W.W. Norton & Co., 1985), 95-96.

[28] Harriet Brent Jacobs, *Incidents in the Life of a Slave Girl,* ed. L. Maria Child (Boston: Act of Congress, 1861), 79.

[29] *Born in Slavery: Slave Narratives from the Federal Writers' Project, 1936-1938, Florida Narratives*, vol. 3, 127.

[30] Deuteronomy 28:30.

[31] La Roy Sunderland, *Anti-slavery Manual: Containing a Collection of Facts and Arguments on American Slavery, Second Edition*. (S.W. Benedict, 1837), 31.

[32] *Born in Slavery: Slave Narratives from the Federal Writers' Project, 1936-1938, Indiana Narratives*, vol. 5, 151.

[33] Arthur W. Calhoun, *A Social History of the American Family From Colonial Times to the Present*, vol. 2 (Cleveland: The Arthur H. Clark Co., 1917), 246.

Chapter 2 The Negro Problem and the Emergence of Eugenics

[1] Abraham Lincoln, John George Nicolay, & John Hay, *Abraham Lincoln: Complete Works, Comprising His Speeches, Letters, State Papers, and Miscellaneous Writings* vol. 1 (New York: The Century Co., 1894), 235.

[2] Marvin T. Wheat, *The Progress and Intelligence of Americans*, 2nd ed. (Louisville: Clerk's Office of the District Court of Kentucky, 1862), 302.

[3] The term "Lynching Century" derived from a Tuskegee Institute study (*Tuskegee Institute Lynching Inventory*) on lynchings between 1882-1968.

[4] Alexis de Tocqueville, ed., John Canfield Spencer, *Democracy in America*, vol. 1 Second American Edition (New York: Aldard and Saunders, 1838), 358.

[5] Alexis de Tocqueville, ed., John Canfield Spencer, *Democracy in America*, vol. 1 4th Edition (New York: Henry G. Langley, 1845), 410.

[6] Jacques-Pierre Brissot de Warville and Étienne Claivè, *New Travels in the United States of America*, Second Edition (London: J.S. Jordan, 1794), 237.

[7] John Hepburn, *American Defense of the Christian Golden Rule: Or an Essay to Prove the Unlawfulness of Making Slaves of Men* (New York?, 1715), 3.

[8] Allen E. Yarema, *American Colonization Society: An Avenue to Freedom?* (New York: University Press of America, 2006), 4.

[9] Thomas Jefferson, *Notes on the State of Virginia* (London: John Stockdale, 1787), 229.

[10] Mia Bay, *The White Image in the Black Mind: African-American Ideas about White People 1830-1925* (New York: Oxford University Press, Inc., 2000), 23.

[11] Gary B. Nash, *Forging Freedom: The Formation of Philadelphia's Black Community 1720-1840* (Cambridge, MA: Harvard University Press, 1988), 237.

[12] James Oliver Horton and Lois E. Horton, *Slavery and the Making of America* (New York: Oxford University Press, 1988), 115.

[13] Robert S. Levine, *Dislocating Race & Nation: Episodes in Nineteenth-Century American Literary Nationalism* (Chapel Hill, NC: University of North Carolina Press, 2008), 82.

[14] Oscar Reiss, *Blacks in Colonial America* (Jefferson, NC: McFarland & Company, Inc., 2006), 154.

[15] Junius P. Rodriguez, *Encyclopedia of Slave Resistance and Rebellion,* vol. 1 (Westport, CT: Greenwood Publishing, 2007), 532.

[16] Frederick Douglass, "Colonization" *North Star,* January 26, 1849, http://utc.iath.virginia.edu/abolitn/abar03at.html.

[17] Julius Eric Thompson, James L. Conyers, and Nancy J. Dawson, *The Frederick Douglass Encyclopedia* (Santa Barbara, CA: Greenwood Publishing, 2010), 157.

[18] Marion Mills Miller, *Great Debates in American History: Slavery from 1790 to 1857* vol. 4 (New York: Current Literature Publishing Company, 1913), 399.

[19] Abraham Lincoln*, Political Speeches and Debates of Abraham Lincoln and S.A. Douglas, 1854-1861* (Battle Creek, MI: International Tract Society, 1895), 458.

[20] Ellis Paxson Oberholtzer, *A History of the United States Since the Civil War: 1865-68* (New York: Macmillan Company, 1917), 76.

[21] Abraham Lincoln and Henry Louis Gates ed., *Lincoln on Race and Slavery* (Princeton, NJ: Princeton University Press, 2009), liii.

[22] Notice of issuance of Proclamation emancipating slaves in States in rebellion on January 1, 1865.

[23] W. Michael Byrd and Linda A. Clayton, *An American Health Dilemma: A Medical History of African Americans and the Problem of Race Beginnings to 1900* (New York: Routledge, 2000), 411.

[24] J. Stahl Patterson, "Increase and Movement of the Colored Population," Popular Science Monthly, XIX (Sept., 1881), 667; Joseph Camp Kennedy, Preliminary Report on the Eighth Census (Washington, DC, 1862), 8.

[25] The Encyclopedia Americana Corporation, *The Encyclopedia Americana: A Library of Universal Knowledge,* vol. 20 (New York: The Encyclopedia Americana Corporation., 1919), 48.

[26] E.W. Gilliam, *The African in the United States The Popular Science Monthly* February vol. 22, no. 28 (New York: D Appleton and Company, February, 1883), 433.

[27] Harriet A. Washington, *Medical Apartheid: The Dark History of Medical Experimentation on Black Americans from Colonial Times to the Present* (New York: Anchor Books, a Division of Random House, 2006), 152.

[28] It was assumed that because Hoffman was of German ancestry that he would be objective in his summation.

[29] Frederick Ludwig Hoffman, *Race Traits and Tendencies of the American Negro* (New York: Macmillan Company, August, 1896), 312.

[30] Southern Society for the Promotion of the Study of Race Conditions and Problems in the South, *Race Problems of the South: Proceedings of the First Annual Conference* (Richmond, VA, 1900), pp. 155-156.

[31] Earl Ofari Hutchinson, The Assassination of the Black Male Image (New York: Simon and Schuster, 1997), 23.

[32] Thomas D. Boston, *A Different Vision Race and Public Policy*, vol. 2 (New York: Routledge, 1997).

[33] Southern Society for the Promotion of the Study of Race Conditions and Problems in the South, *Race Problems of the South: Proceedings of the First Annual Conference* (Richmond, VA, 1900), 155-156.

[34] Joseph Alexander Tillinghast, *The Negro in America and Africa* vol. 3, Issue 2 of American Economic Association, Publications, 3rd Series (New York: Macmillan Company, 1902), 95-96.

[35] Howard Winant, *The World is a Ghetto: Race and Democracy Since World War II* (New York: Basic Books, 2001), 107-108.

[36] Ernst Cassirer, *The Myth of the State* (New Haven, Conn: Yale University Press, 1974), 228.

[37] John P. Jackson and Nadine M. Weidman, *Race, Racism, and Science: Social Impact and Interaction* (Santa Barbara, Calif.: Rutgers University Press, 2004), 107.

[38] Francis Galton, *Memories of My Life* (London: Methuen & Co., 1908), 287.

[39] Charles Darwin, *The Descent of Man, and Selection in Relation to Sex,* vol. 1 (New York: D. Appleton and Company, 1871), 161-162.

[40] Francis Galton, *Hereditary Genius: An Inquiry Into Its Laws and Consequences* (London: Macmillan and Co., 1869), 1.

[41] Francis Galton, *Inquiries into Human Faculty and Its Development* (London: Macmillan and Co.: 1883), 24-25.

[42] Charles Darwin and Francis Darwin, ed., *The Life and Letters of Charles Darwin: Including an Autobiographical Chapter,* vol. 2 (New York: D. Appleton and Co., 1896), 294

[43] Charles Darwin, *The Descent of Man, and Selection in Relation to Sex,* vol. 1 (New York: D. Appleton and Company, 1871), 201.

[44] Francis Galton, *The Possible Improvement of the Human Breed Under the Existing Conditions of Law and Sentiment*, in Norman Lockyear Nature: A Weekly Illustrated Journal of Science vol. LXIV (New York: Macmillan and Co. Oct 31, 1901), 659.

[45] Madison Grant, *The Passing of the Great Race or the Racial Basis of European History* (New York: Charles Scribner's Sons, 1916), 18.

[46] Havelock Ellis, "The World's Racial Problems" *Birth Control Review* (October, 1920), 16.

Chapter 3 The Harlem Project and the Legacy of Margaret Sanger

[1] Ellis Havelock, "The World's Racial Problem" *Birth Control Review*: (October 1920)14-16.

[2] National Association for the Advancement of Colored People, ed., W.E.B. Du Bois, *The Crisis* "Opinion," (New York: Crisis Publishing. Co., 1921), 248.

[3] Carole Ruth McCann, *Birth Control Politics in the United States, 1916-1945* (Ithaca, New York: Cornell University Press, 1999), 139.

[4] Gwendolyn Mink and Alice O' Connor, *Poverty in the United States: An Encyclopedia of History, Politics, and Poverty in the United States* vol. 1. (Santa Barbara, Calif.: ABC-CLIO, Inc., 2004) 61.

[5] Hamilton Cravens and Peter C. Mancall, *Great Depression: People and Perspectives* (Santa Barbara, Calif.: Greenwood Publishing Group, 2009), 123.

[6] Hamilton Cravens and Peter C. Mancall, *Great Depression: People and Perspectives*, 123.

[7] Clovis E. Semmes, Racism, Health, and Post-industrialism: A Theory of African-American Health (Santa Barbara, Calif.: Greenwood Publishing Group, 1996), 57.

[8] Harriet A. Washington, *Medical Apartheid: The Dark History of Medical Experimentation on Black Americans from Colonial Times to the Present* (New York: Anchor Books, a Division of Random House, 2006), 197.

[9] Sana Loue, *Textbook of Research Ethics: Theory and Practice* (New York: Springer-Verlag, 2000), 6.

[10] W.EB Du Bois, "Black Folk and Birth Control." *Birth Control Review*. (June, 1932): 166.

[11] W.EB Du Bois, "Black Folk and Birth Control.", 166.

[12] Harriet A. Washington, *Medical Apartheid: The Dark History of Medical Experimentation on Black Americans from Colonial Times to the Present* (New York: Anchor Books, a Division of Random House, 2006), 197.

[13] Margaret Sanger's December 19, 1939 letter to Dr. Clarence Gamble, 255 Adams Street, Milton, Massachusetts. North Hampton, Mass.: Sophia Smith Collection, Smith College.

[14] Washington, *Medical Apartheid: The Dark History of Medical Experimentation on Black Americans from Colonial Times to the Present*, 197.

Chapter 4 The Rhineland "Bastardes"

[1] Alfred Ploetz, A. Nordenholz, and Ludwig Plate, *Archiv für Rassen- und Geesellscaftsbiologie,* vol. 1 (Berlin: Verlag der Archiv-Gesellschaft, Berlin SW. 12., 1904), 1.

[2] Gretchen E. Schafft, *From Racism to Genocide: Anthropology in the Third Reich* (Champaign, Ill: University of Illinois Press, 2004), 43.

[3] The first *Konzentrationslager* or concentration camps were in Namibia, and it was here where Eugen Fischer also conducted genocidal experiments on Herero prisoners of war. This was the pretext of the holocaust.

[4] Clarence Lusane, *Hitler's Black Victims: The Historical Experiences of Afro Germans, European Blacks, Africans, and African Americans in the Nazi Era* (New York: Routledge, 2003), 45.

[5] A. Dirk Moses, *Empire, Colony Genocide: Conquest, Occupation, and Subalteran Resistance in World History* (New York: Berghahn Books, 2008), 38.

[6] Clarence Lusane, *Hitler's Black Victims: The Historical Experiences of Afro Germans, European Blacks, Africans, and African Americans in the Nazi Era*, 127.

[7] Tina M. Campt, *Other Germans: Black Germans and the Politics of Race, Gender, and Memory in the Third Reich Social History, Popular Culture, and Politics in Germany* (Ann Arbor: University of Michigan Press, 2005), 73.

[8] Stefan Kühl, *The Nazi Connection: Eugenics, American Racism, and German National Socialism* (New York: Oxford University Press, 2002), 192.

[9] *Buck v. Bell*, 274 U.S. 200 (1927).

[10] Timothy W. Ryback, *Hitler's Private Library: The Books That Shaped His Life* (New York: First Vintage Books, 2010), 115.

[11] Cyprian Blamires, *World Fascism: A Historical Encyclopedia*, vol. 1 (Santa Barbara, Calif.: ABC-CLIO, 2006), 207.

Chapter 5 The Mississippi Appendectomy

[1] See Chapter 4 *"The Rhineland Bastardes" of Germany.*

[2] *Buck v. Bell*, 274 U.S. 200 (1927).

[3] *Relf et al. vs. Weinberger et. al.* Civil Action No. 73-1557 U.S. District Court. Washington, D.C., March 15, 1974.

[4] Harriet A. Washington, *Medical Apartheid: The Dark History of Medical Experimentation on Black Americans from Colonial Times to the Present* (New York: Anchor Books, a Division of Random House, 2006), 204.

[5] Student Nonviolent Coordinating Committee, *Genocide in Mississippi Atlanta*: Manuscript, Archives, and Rare Book Library, Emory University, 2006. Accessed December 28, 2011. http://www.delta.com/about_delta/investor_relations/annual_report_p roxy_stat ement/.

[6] Carl M. Cobb, "Students Charge BCH's Obstetrics Unit with 'Excessive Surgery'," *Boston Globe*, Apr. 29, 1972,

[7] Robert E. McGarrah, *Voluntary Female Sterilization: Abuses, Risks and Guidelines*. Hastings Center Reports vol. 4 no. 3 (The Hastings Center: June 1974), 5-7.

Chapter 6 Teens, "Welfare Queens", and "Crack Mommas" Need Birth Control

[1] Stanlie Myrise James and Abena P. Busia, *Theorizing Black Feminisms: The Visionary Pragmatism of Black Women* (New York: Routledge, 1993), 158

[2] Donald Kimmelman, "Poverty and Norplant: Can Contraception Reduce the Underclass?," *Philadelphia Inquirer*, Dec. 12, 1990.

³ Tamar Lewin, "A Plan to Pay Welfare Mothers for Birth Control", *New York Times*, Feb. 09, 1991.

⁴ "Incentive Offered for Birth Control" *Star News*, Apr. 17, 1992.

⁵ Rebecca Kavoussi, "Norplant and the Dark Side of the Law," *Washington Free Press*, Mar./Apr. 1997.

⁶ Allen C. Soong, "The Use and Abuse of Norplant," *Harvard Crimson*, Feb. 08, 1993.

⁷ Kimberly Wallace-Sanders, *Skin Deep, Spirit Strong: The Black Female Body in American Culture* (Ann Arbor: University of Michigan Press, 2002), 289.

⁸ National Center for Biotechnology Information, U.S. National Library of Medicine "Clinicians, Patients, Medicaid: Is Anyone to Blame for Norplant Removal Dilemma? Part II," *Contraceptive Technology Update* vol. 14, no. 10 (Oct, 1993): 149-153.

⁹ Stephanie J. Ventura, Joyce C. Abma, William D. Mosher, and Stanley K. Henshaw, *Center for Disease Control Recent Trends in Teenage Pregnancy in the United States, 1990-2002* Hyattsville, MD: National Center for Health Statistics, Dec. 13, 2006.

¹⁰ Harriet A. Washington, *Medical Apartheid: The Dark History of Medical Experimentation on Black Americans from Colonial Times to the Present* (New York: Anchor Books , a Division of Random House, 2006), 207-208.

¹¹ United States Congress House Committee on Small Business. *Subcommittee on Regulation, Business Opportunities and Technology, Norplant and Contraceptive Pricing: Conflict of Interest, Protection of Public Ownership in Drug Development Deals Between Tax-Exempt, Federally Supported Labs and the Pharmaceutical Industry: Hearing Before the Subcommittee on Small Business, House of Representatives, One Hundred Third Congress, First Session* (Washington U.S. G.P.O., 1994).

¹² Depo-Provera has been used to limit the birth rate black populations around the globe. For instance, the apartheid government of South Africa used Depo-Provera to significantly curtail the working black population. Mobile clinics traveled through the country side providing birth control while free injections where offered at many

factories. Often women risked being fired if they refused the contraception. A study in France revealed that of female birth control users that used Depo-Provera only 4% were French born, while 15% were Algerian, and 20% Sub Saharan women. This was true in spite of the fact that African women were up to two times more likely to request another type of contraception. Similar disproportions in Depo-Provera between the Ethiopians and Israelis living in Israel are evident. During the 1980's, approximately 90,000 Ethiopians were immigrated to Israel under the Laws of Return. Today, they face extreme discrimination in the areas of employment, housing, and education. There seems to be an unwritten government policy to decrease their numbers. It is estimated that although the Ethiopian Beta Israel community are 1.75% of the total population, according to data from Clalit they make up 57% of all Depo-Provera users in Israel.

[13] National Black Women's Health Project, ed. Linda Villarosa, *Body & Soul: The Black Women's Guide to Physical Health and Emotional Well-Being* (New York: HarperPerennial, 1994), 169.

[14] Charles S. Morrison, et al. "Hormonal Contraceptive use, Cervical Ectopy, and the Acquisition of Cervical Infections," *Sexually Transmitted Diseases* vol. 31, no. 9 (Sept. 2004): 561-567.

[15] Charles S. Morrison and Kavita Nanda, "Hormonal Contraception and HIV: An Unanswered Question" *Lancet Infections Diseases*, vol. 12 no. 1 (Jan. 2012), 2-3.

Chapter 7 Black Leadership and Birth Control: From Garvey to Obama

[1] Amy Jacques-Garvey, *The Philosophy & Opinions of Marcus Garvey or Africa For the Africans* (Dover: The Majority Press, 1986), 348.

[2] Charles S. Johnson, "A Question of Negro Health," (June 1932): 167-169.

[3] E. Franklin Frazier, "The Negro and Birth Control," *Birth Control Review* vol. 17, no. 8 (March, 1933):68-70.

[4] Julian Lewis, "Can the Negro Afford Birth Control," *Negro Digest* 3 (May, 1945): 19-22.

[5] Elijah Muhammad, "The Safety of the Black Man in the World Revolution" *Muhammad Speaks*, July 23, 1965.

[6] Evette Pearson, "In White America Today" *Black Panther*, Jan. 4, 1969.

[7] Jesse L. Jackson to Thea Barron, (Sept. 6, 1977) A Telegram printed in the Congressional Recorded vol. 123, pt. 24, 31038.

[8] Jesse L. Jackson "How Shall We Regard Life?" Right to Life News (January, 1977).

[9] Paul Taylor, Rakesh Kochhar, Richard Fry, and Seth Motel, *Twenty-to-One: Wealth Gaps Rise to Record Highs Between Whites, Blacks, and Hispanics* (Tuesday, July 26, 2011).

[10] Paul R. Ehrlich, John P. Holdren, & Anne H. Ehrlich, *Ecoscience: Population, Resources, Environment* (W.H. Freeman & Co., 3rd Edition, 1978).

[11] NARAL Pro-Choice America, formerly known as National Association for the Repeal of Abortion Laws then National Abortion Rights Action League, and later National Abortion and Reproductive Rights League.

Chapter 8 Roe v. Wade: A Wrong Decision

[1] *Doe v. Bolton* extended the right to have an abortion through any month of pregnancy.

[2] R.K. Jones and K. Kooistra, Abortion Incidence and Access to Services in the United States, 2008 Perspectives on Sexual and Reproductive Health, 2011 vol. 43 no. 1, 41-50.

[3] Dissenting opinion in Akron v. Akron Center for Reproductive Health, quoting Chief Justice Warren Burger's dissent in Plyler v. Doe, 457 U.S. 202 1982.

[4] *Roe v. Wade*, 410 U.S. 113 - 1973.

[5] Report, Subcommittee on Separation of Powers to Senate Judiciary Committee S-158, 97th Congress, 1st Congress, 1st Session 1981, 7.

[6] The word "trimester" was not a medical term prior to *Roe v. Wade* and *Doe v. Bolton*.

[7] *Webster v. Reproductive Health Services*, 492 U.S. 490 1989.

[8] Viability refers to the time a fetus is able to survive outside of the womb.
[9] *Doe v. Bolton*, 410 U.S. 179, 1973.
[10] English case laws that set legal standards
[11] *Roe v. Wade*, 410 U.S. 113 - 1973.
[12] Edward Coke was the authority on common law during the 17th century.
[13] John Keown, *Abortion, Doctors and the Law: Some Aspects of the Legal Regulation of Abortion in England from 1803 to 1982* (New York: Cambridge University Press, 2002), 10.
[14] *Roe v. Wade*, 410 U.S. 113 - 1973.
[15] William Blackstone, Edward Christian, John Frederic Archbold, Joseph Chitty and Barron Field, *Commentaries on the Laws of England, Sir William Blackstone* vol. 1 (New York: E. Duyckinck, 1827), 94.
[16] Robert M. Byrn, "An American Tragedy: The Supreme Court on Abortion," *Fordham Law Review* 41, 4 (1973): 22.
[17] Emily Bazelon, "The Place of Women on the Court" *New York Times Magazine*, July 7, 2009.
[18] Brief for the United States as Amicus Curiae, Brown v. Board of Education, 347 U.S. 483 (1954).

Chapter 9 Biblical Argument Against Abortion

[19] Psalms 139:13-16.
[20] Genesis 2:7.
[21] Job 31:14-15.
[22] Isaiah 44:24.
[23] Jeremiah 1:5.
[24] Galatians 1:15-16.
[25] Luke 1:15.
[26] Genesis 1:28.
[27] From the beginning children were to be born within the confines of marriage. Nevertheless, this does not justify the arbitrary killing of children born out-of-wedlock.
[28] Exodus 20:13.

[29] Lawrence B. Finer et al., Lori F. Frohwirth, Lindsay A. Dauphinee, Susheela Singh, and Ann M. Moore, "Reasons U.S. Women Have Abortions: Quantitative and Qualitative Perspectives," *Perspectives on Sexual and Reproductive Health*, vol. 37, No. 3, (2005):110-118.
[30] Ezekiel 18:19.
[31] Ezekiel 18:20.
[32] Deuteronomy 24:16.
[33] Psalms 82:6.
[34] John 10:34-36.
[35] Philippians 3:20-21.
[36] Daniel 12:3.
[37] William Edward Harrtpole, Lecky, *History of European Morals, From Augustus to Charlemagne* vol. 2 (London: Longams, Green, and Co., 1869), 22.

Chapter 10 Sacrificing Our Future (An Appeal to Conscience)

[1] U.S. Department of Health and Human Services Centers for Disease Control and Prevention National Center for HIV/AIDs, Viral Hepatitis, STD, and TB Prevention Division of STD Prevention, *Sexual Transmitted Disease Surveillance, 2009*, November, 2010.

[2] U.S. Department of Health and Human Services Centers for Disease Control and Prevention National Center for HIV/AIDs, Viral Hepatitis, STD, and TB Prevention Division of STD Prevention, *Sexual Transmitted Disease Surveillance, 2009*, November, 2010.

[3] U.S. Teen Birth Rate Fell to Record Low in 2009 Still, more than 400,000 teen girls give birth each year in the United States. April 5, 2011.

[4] Researchers collected data on 838 females aged 14-19 who took part in a 2003-2004 Health and Nutrition Examination Study. (This study did not include HIV, gonorrhea, or syphilis.)

[5] Center For Disease Control, National Center for HIV/AIDS, Hepatitis, STD, and TB Prevention Division of HIV/AIDS Prevention, *HIV among African Americans*. September, 2010.

[6] Joy Jones, "Marriage Is for White People," *The Washington Post*, Mar. 26, 2006.

[7] Cassandra Dorious, *Reconceptualizing Family Instability to Include Measures of Childbearing: The Practical Value of Assessing Multiple Partner Fertility*, Washington D.C.: Population Association of America Annual Meetings, March 31-April 2, 2011. Population Association of America.

[8] Susan A. Cohen, "Abortion and Women of Color: The Bigger Picture," *Guttmacher Policy Review* 11, no. 3 (Summer, 2008).

[9] Department of Health and Human Services Centers for Disease Control and Prevention, *Morbidity and Mortality Weekly Report* vol. 58, no. 22-28 (November 27, 2009), 22.

[10] Statistical Analysis and Reporting and Quality Improvement Units of the Bureau of Vital Statistics New York City Department of Health and Mental Hygiene, *Summary of Vital Statistics 2010 The City of New York Pregnancy Outcomes*.

[11] The Guttmacher Institute provides a more comprehensive estimate of abortion rates.

[12] Jones R.K., Finer L.B., and Singh S., Characteristics of U.S. Abortion Patients, 2008, New York: Guttmacher Institute, 2010.

[13] Melonie Heron, Division of Vital Statistics, "Deaths: Leading Causes for 2006," *National Vital Statistics Reports* vol. 58 no. 14 (March 31, 2010): 7.

BIBLIOGRAPHY

American Cotton Planter and the Soil of the South, vol. 1. Montgomery, Ala.: Underwood & Cloud, 1857.

Bacon, Leonard, *Slavery Discussed in Occasional Essays From 1833-1846*. New York: Baker and Scribner, 1846.

Bay, Mia. *The White Image in the Black Mind: African-American Ideas about White People 1830-1925*. New York: Oxford University Press, Inc., 2000.

Bazelon, Emily. "The Place of Women on the Court" *New York Times Magazine*, July 7, 2009.

Berlin, Ira. *Many Thousands Gone: The First Two Centuries of Slavery in NorthAmerica*. United States: Harvard University Press, 1998.

Blackstone, Wiliam, Christian, Edward, Archbold, John Frederic, Chitty, Joseph and Field Barron. *Commentaries on the Laws of England, Sir William Blackstone* vol. 1. New York: E. Duyckinck, 1827.

Born in Slavery: *Slave Narratives from the Federal Writers' Project, 1936-1938*. Wash., D.C.: Library of Congress, 2001. <memory.loc.gov/amm em/snhtml/snhome.html> (16 December 2011).

Boston, Thomas. *A Different Vision Race and Public Policy*, vol. 2 New York: Routledge, 1997.

Blamires, Cyprian. *World Fascism: A Historical Encyclopedia*, vol. 1. Santa Barbara, Calif.: ABC-CLIO, 2006.

Brief for the United States as Amicus Curiae, Brown v. Board of Education, 347 U.S. 483 (1954).

Brissot de Warville, Jacques-Pierre and Claivè, Étienne. *New Travels in the United States of America*, Second Edition, London: J.S. Jordan, 1794.

Buck v. Bell, 274 U.S. 200 (1927)

Byrd, W. Michael and Clayton Linda A. *An American Health Dilemma: A Medical History of African Americans and the Problem of Race Beginnings to 1900*. New York: Routledge, 2000.

Byrn, Robert, M. "An American Tragedy: The Supreme Court on Abortion." *Fordham Law Review* vol. 41, 4 (1973): 22.

Calhoun, Arthur W. *A Social History of the American Family From Colonial Times to the Present*, vol. 2. Cleveland: The Arthur H. Clark Co., 1917.

Campt, Tina, M. Other Germans: *Black Germans and the Politics of Race, Gender, and Memory in the Third Reich Social History, Popular Culture, and Politics in Germany*. Ann Arbor: University of Michigan Press, 2005.

Cassirer, Ernst. *The Myth of the State*. New Haven, Conn.: Yale University Press, 1974.

Center for Disease Control. Recent Trends in Teenage Pregnancy in the United States,1990-2002. (Hyattsville MD: National Center for Health Statistics, 2006): 207-208.

Center For Disease Control National Center for HIV/AIDS, Hepatitis, STD, and TB Prevention Division of HIV/AIDS Prevention. *HIV among African Americans*. September, 2010.

"Clinicians, Patients, Medicaid: Is Anyone to Blame for Norplant Removal Dilemma? Part II." *Contraceptive Technology Update* vol. 14, no. 10 October 1993): 149-153.

Cobb, Carl, M. "Students Charge BCH's Obstetrics Unit with Excessive Surgery". Boston Globe, Apr. 29, 1972.

Cohen, Susan, A. "Abortion and Women of Color: The Bigger Picture." *Guttmacher Policy Review* vol. 11, no. 3 (Summer, 2008).

Conrad, A.H. & Meyer, J.R., *The Economics of Slavery in the Antebellum South and Other Studies in Econometric History*. Piscataway, N.J.: Aldine Publishing Company, 1964.

Cooper, Thomas Valentine and Fenton, Hector Tyndale. *American Politics (non-partisan) From the Beginning to the End*. Chicago: C.R. Brodix, 1884.

Cravens, Hamilton and Mancall, Peter C. *Great Depression: People and Perspectives*. Santa Barbara, Calif.: Greenwood Publishing Group, 2009.

Department of Commerce and Labor Bureau of the Census, *A Century of Population Growth: From the First Census of the United states to the Twelfth 1790-1900*. Washington D.C.: Government Printing Office, 1909.

Darwin, Charles. *The Descent of Man, and Selection in Relation to Sex*, vol. 1. New York: D. Appleton and Co., 1871.

Darwin, Charles and Darwin, Francis, ed. *The Life and Letters of Charles Darwin: Including an Autobiographical Chapter*, vol. 2. New York: D. Appleton and Co., 1896.

Department of Health and Human Services Centers for Disease Control and Prevention. *Morbidity and Mortality Weekly Report* vol. 58, no. 22-28 (November 27, 2009): 22.

Doe v. Bolton, 410 U.S. 179, 1973.

Dorious, Cassandra. *Reconceptualizing Family Instability to Include Measures of Childbearing: The Practical Value of Assessing Multiple Partner Fertility*. Presented at Population Association of America Annual Meetings, March 31- April 2, 2011. Wash. D.C.: Population Association of America.

Du Bois, W.E.B. "Black Folk and Birth Control." *Birth Control Review*. (June, 1932): 166.

Douglas, Frederick. "Colonization." *North Star*. (January 26, 1849).

Gates, Henry Louis. *Lincoln on Race and Slavery*. Princeton, N.J.: Princeton University Press, 2009.

Douglas, Frederick., *Narrative of the Life of Frederick Douglass*. New York: Dover Publications, Inc., 1995.

Ellis, Havelock. "The World's Racial Problem" *Birth Control Review* (October, 1920): 14-16.

Encyclopedia Americana Corporation, *The Encyclopedia Americana: A Library of Universal Knowledge*, vol. 20. New York: D. Appleton and Co., February, 1883.

Galton, Francis. *Hereditary Genius: An Inquiry Into Its Laws and Consequences*. London: Macmillan and Co., 1869.

------. *Inquiries into Human Faculty and Its Development*. London: Macmillan and Co., 1883.

------. *The Possible Improvement of the Human Breed Under the Existing Conditions of Law and Sentiment*, in Norman Lockyear *Nature: A Weekly Illustrated Journal of Science* vol. LXIV. New York: Macmillan and Co., 1901.

------. *Memories of My Life*. London: Methuen & Co., 1908.

Goodell, William. *The American Slave Code in Theory and Practice: Its Distinctive Features Shown by Its Statutes, Judicial Decisions, and Illustrative Facts*. New York: American and Foreign Anti-Slavery Society, 1853.

Grant, Madison. *The Passing of the Great Race or the Racial Basis of European History*. New York: Charles Scribner's Sons, 1916.

Gutman, Herbert George. *The Black Family in Slavery and Freedom, 1750-1925*. New York: Pantheon Books, 1976.

Grandy, Moses. *Narrative of the Life of Moses Grandy, Late a Slave in the United States of America*. Boston: O. Johnson Publishing Co., 1844.

Hepburn, John. *American Defense of the Christian Golden Rule: Or an Essay to Prove the Unlawfulness of Making Slaves of Men*. New York?.: s.n., 1715.

Heron, Melonie, Division of Vital Statistics "Deaths: Leading Causes for 2006." *National Vital Statistics Reports* vol. 58, no. 14 (March 31, 2010): 7.

Hoffman, Frederick Ludwig. *Race Traits and Tendencies of the American Negro*. New York: Macmillan Co., August, 1896.

Holy Bible King, James Version.

Horton, James Oliver, Horton, Lois E. *Slavery and the Making of America*. New York: Oxford University Press, 1988.

Hutchinson, Earl Ofari. *The Assassination of the Black Male Image*. New York: Simon and Schuster, 1997.

"Incentive Offered for Birth Control." *Star News*, Apr. 17, 1992.

Israel, Elisha J. *Into Egypt Again With Ships: A Message to the Forgotten Israelites* (African Americans). United States: CreateSpace, 2009.

Jackson, Jesse. Jesse L. *Jackson to Thea Barron, A Telegram printed in the Congressional Recorded*, vol. 123, pt. 24, 31038.

Jackson, John P. and Weidman, Nadine. M. *Race, Racism, and Science: Social Impact and Interaction*. Santa Barbara, Calif. Rutgers University Press, 2004.

Jacobs, Harriet Brent. *Incidents in the Life of a Slave Girl*, ed. L. Maria Child. Boston: Act of Congress, 1861.

Jacques-Garvey, Amy. *The Philosophy & Opinions of Marcus Garvey or Africa for the Africans*. Dover: The Majority Press, 1986.

James, Stanlie Myrise and Busia, Abena P. *Theorizing Black Feminisms: The Visionary Pragmatism of Black Women*. New York: Routledge, 1993.

Jefferson, Thomas. *Notes on the State of Virginia*. London: John Stockdale, 1787.

Johnson, Charles, S. "The Negro and Birth Control." *Birth Control Review* vol. 17, no. 8 (March, 1933): 68-70.

Jones, Joy. "Marriage Is for White People," *The Washington Post*, Mar. 26, 2006.

Jones, R.K., Finer, L.B., Singh, S. *Characteristics of U.S. Abortion Patients, 2008*. New York: Guttmacher Institute, 2010.

Kavoussi, Rebecca. "Norplant and the Dark Side of the Law." *Washington Free Press*, Mar./Apr. 1997.

Keown, John. *Abortion, Doctors and the Law: Some Aspects of the Legal Regulation of Abortion in England from 1803 to 1982*. New York: Cambridge University Press, 2002.

Kimmelman, Donald. "Poverty and Norplant: Can Contraception Reduce the Underclass?." *Philadelphia Inquirer*, Dec. 12, 1990.

Kühl, Stefan. *The Nazi Connection: Eugenics, American Racism, and German National Socialism*. New York: Oxford University Press, 2002.

Lecky, William Edward Hartpole. *History of European Morals, From Augustus to Charlemagne* vol. 2. London: Longams, Green, and Co., 1869.

Levine, Robert S. *Dislocating Race & Nation: Episodes in Nineteenth-Century American Literary Nationalism*. Chapel Hill, N.C.: University of North Carolina Press, 2008.

Lewin, Tamar. "A Plan to Pay Welfare Mothers for Birth Control." *New York Times*, Feb. 09, 1991.

Lewis, Julian. "Can the Negro Afford Birth Control." *Negro Digest* 3 (May, 1945): 19-22.

Lincoln, Abraham. *Abraham Lincoln: Complete Works, Comprising His Speeches, Letters, State Papers, and Miscellaneous Writings* vol. 1. Edited by John George Nicolay and John Hay. New York: The Century Co., 1894.

Lincoln, Abraham. *Political Speeches and Debates of Abraham Lincoln and S.A. Douglass 1854-1861*. Edited by Alonzo T. Jones. New York: Macmillan Company, 1917.

Loue, Sana. *Textbook of Research Ethics: Theory and Practice*. New York: Springer-Verlag, 2000.

Lusane, Clarence. *Hitler's Black Victims: The Historical Experiences of Afro Germans, European Blacks, Africans, and African Americans in the Nazi Era*. New York: Routledge, 2003.

McCann, Carole R. *Birth Control Politics in the United States, 19916-1945*. Ithaca, New York: Cornell University Press, 1999.

McGarrah, Robert E. *Voluntary Female Sterilization: Abuses, Risks and Guidelines*. Hastings Center Reports vol. 4, no. 3 (The Hastings Center: June, 1974), 5-7.

Miller, Marion Mills. *Great Debates in American History: Slavery from 1790 to 1857* vol. 4. New York: Current Literature Publishing Company, 1913.

Mink, Gwendolyn and O'Connor, Alice. *Poverty in the United States: An Encyclopedia of History, Politics, and Poverty in the United States* vol. 1. Santa Barbara, Calif.: ABC-CLIO, Inc., 2004.

Moore, Ann, M. "Reasons U.S. Women Have Abortions: Quantitative and Qualitative Perspectives," *Perspectives on Sexual and Reproductive Health*, vol. 37, No. 3, (2005):110-118.

Morrison, C.S., Bright P., Wong, EL, Kwok, C., Yacobson, I., Gaydos, C.A., Tucker H.T., and Blumenthal, P.D. "Hormonal Contraceptive use, Cervical Ectopy, and the Acquisition of Cervical Infections," *Sexually Transmitted Diseases* vol. 31, no. 9 (Sept. 2004): 561-567.

Morrison, C.S. and Kavita Nanda. "Hormonal Contraception and HIV: An Unanswered Question " *Lancet Infections Diseases*, vol. 12, no. 1 (Jan. 2012), 2-3.

Moses, Dirk A. *Empire Colony Genocide: Conquest, Occupation, and Subalteran Resistance in World History*. New York: Berghahn Books, 2008.

Muhammad, Elijah. "The Safety of the Black Man in the World Revolution" *Muhammad Speaks*, July 23, 1965.

Mydral, Gunnar. *An American Dilemma: The Negro Problem and Modern Democracy*. New York: Harper & Brothers, 1944.

Nash, Gary, B. *Forging Freedom: The Formation of Philadelphia's Black Community 1720-1840*. Cambridge, Mass: Harvard University Press, 1988.

National Black Women's Health Project, ed. Villarosa, Linda. *Body & Soul: The Black Women's Guide to Physical Health and Emotional Well-Being*. New York: HarperPerennial, 1994.

National Association for the Advancement of Colored Peopled, ed., W.E.B. Du Bois. *The Crisis*. vols. 22-24. New York: Crisis Publishing. Co., 1921.

Oberholtzer, Ellis Paxson. *A History of the United States Since the Civil War: 1865-68*. New York: Macmillan Company, 1917.

Olmstead, Frederick Law, *Journey and Explorations in the Cotton Kingdom*, vol. 1. London: S. Low, Son & Co., 1861.

Patterson, J. Stahl. "Increase and Movement of the Colored Population." *Popular Science Monthly*, XIX (Sept., 1881), 667; Joseph Camp Kennedy, *Preliminary Report on the Eighth Census*: Washington, D.C., 1862.

Pearson, Evette. "In White America Today." *Black Panther*, Jan. 4, 1969.

Ploetz, Alfred, Nordenholz, A. and Plate, Ludwig. *Archiv für Rassen- und Geesellscaftsbiologie,* vol. 1. Berlin: Verlag der Archiv-Gesellschaft, Berlin SW. 12, 1904.

Relf et al. vs. Weinberger et al. Civil Action No. 73-1557 U.S. District Court. Washington, D.C.: March 15, 1974.

Reiss, Oscar. *Blacks in Colonial America.* Jefferson, N.C.: McFarland & Company, Inc., 2006.

Roberts, Dorothy. *Killing the Black Body.* New York: Pantheon Books, a division of Random House, Inc., 1997.

Rodriguez, Junius, P. *Encyclopedia of Slave Resistance and Rebellion,* vol. 1. Westport, Conn.: Greenwood Publishing, 2007.

------. *Slavery in the United States: A Social, Political, and Historical Encyclopedia,* vol. 1. ABC-CLIO: Santa Barbara, Calif., 2007.

Roe v. Wade, 410 U.S. 113 - 1973.

Ryback, Timothy, W. *Hitler's Private Library: The Books That Shaped His Life.* New York: First Vintage Books, 2010.

Sands, Samuel. *The American Farmer, and Spirit of the Agricultural Journals of the Day,Devoted to the Interests of the Farmers, Planters & Horticulturists of the United States.* Baltimore: Samuel Sands, Publisher, 1848.

Schafft, Gretchen E. *From Racism to Genocide: Anthropology in the Third Reich.* Champaign, Ill: University of Illinois Press, 2004.

Southern Society for the Promotion of the Study of Race Conditions and Problems in the South. Race Problems of the South: *Proceedings of the First Annual Conference.* Richmond, Va., 1900.

Sanger, Margaret. December 19, 1939 letter to Dr. Clarence Gamble 255 Adams Street, Milton, Massachusetts. North Hampton, Mass.: Sophia Smith Collection, Smith College.

Single Black Female. *Night Line ABC News.* December 23, 2009.

Soong, Allen C. "The Use and Abuse of Norplant." *Harvard Crimson,* Feb. 8, 1993.

Statistical Analysis and Reporting and Quality Improvement Units of the Bureau of Vital Statistics New York City Department of Health and Mental Hygiene, *Summary of Vital Statistics, 2010 The City of New York Pregnancy Outcomes.*

Student Nonviolent Coordinating Committee. *Genocide in Mississippi Atlanta.* Manuscript, Archives, and Rare Book Library, Emory University, 2006.

Subcommittee on Separation of Powers to Senate Judiciary Committee. Report, Subcommittee on Separation of Powers to Senate Judiciary Committee S-158, 97th Congress, 1st Congress, 1st Session, 1981.

Sunderland, La Roy. *Anti-slavery Manual: Containing a Collection of Facts and Arguments on American Slavery*, 2nd ed. New York: S.W. Benedict, 1837.

Taylor, Paul, Kochhar, Rakesh, Fry, Richard, and Motel Seth. *Twenty to One: Wealth Gaps Rise toRecord Highs Between Whites, Blacks, and Hispanics.* Pew Research Center, July 26, 2011.

Thompson, Julius Eric, Conyers, James L., and Dawson, Nancy J. *The Frederick Douglas Encyclopedia.* Santa Barbara, Calif.: Greenwood Publishing, 2010.

Tillinghast, Joseph Alexander. *The Negro in America and Africa* vol. 3, Issue 2 of American Economic Association, Publications, 3rd Series. New York: Macmillan Company, 1902.

Tocqueville, Alexis de., ed., Spencer, John Canfield. *Democracy in America*, vol. 1 Second American Edition. New York: Aldard and Saunders, 1838.

------. *Democracy in America*, vol. 1 4th ed. American Edition. New York: Henry G. Langley, 1845.

United States Bureau of Census, *Preliminary Report on the Eighth Census, 1860, of the United States.* Washington D.C.: Government Printing Office, 1862.

U.S. Department of Health and Human Services Centers for Disease Control and Prevention National Center for HIV/AIDs, Viral Hepatitis, STD, and TB Prevention Division of STD Prevention, *Sexual Transmitted Disease Surveillance, 2009.* November, 2010.

Wallace-Sanders, Kimberly. *Skin Deep, Spirit Strong: The Black Female Body in American Culture.* Ann Arbor: University of Michigan Press, 2002.

Washington, Harriet A. *Medical Apartheid: The Dark History of Medical Experimentation on Black Americans from Colonial Times to the Present.* New York: Anchor Books , a Division of Random House, 2006.

Webster v. Reproductive Health Services, 492 U.S. 490 1989.

Weld, Theodore Dwight. *American Slavery, As It Is: Testimony of a Thousand Witnesses.* New York: American Anti-Slavery Society, 1839.

Wheat, Marvin, T. *The Progress and Intelligence of Americans*, 2nd ed. Louisville: Office of the District Court of Kentucky, 1862.

White, Deborah Gray. *Ar'nt I a Woman?: Female Slaves in Plantation South.* New York: W.W. Norton & Co., 1985.

Winant, Howard. *The World is a Ghetto: Race and Democracy Since World War II.* New York: Basic Books, 2001.

United States Congress House Committee on Small Business. *Subcommittee on Regulation, Business Opportunities and Technology, Norplant and Contraceptive Pricing: Conflict of Interest, Protection of Public Ownership in Drug Development Deals Between Tax-Exempt, Federally Supported Labs and the Pharmaceutical Industry: Hearing Before the Subcommittee on Small Business, House of Representatives, One Hundred Third Congress, First Session.* Wash., D.C.: U.S. G.P.O., 1994.

Vital Statistics New York City Department of Health and Mental Hygiene, *Summary of Vital Statistics 2010 The City of New York Pregnancy Outcomes.*

Yarema, Allen, E. *American Colonization Society: An Avenue to Freedom?* New York: University Press of America, 2006.

Made in the USA
Lexington, KY
01 December 2016